Fostering a Child's Recovery
Family Placement for Traumatized Children

Mike Thomas and Terry Philpot

Foreword by Mary Walsh

Jessica Kingsley Publishers
London and Philadelphia

First published in 2009
by Jessica Kingsley Publishers
116 Pentonville Road
London N1 9JB, UK
and
400 Market Street, Suite 400
Philadelphia, PA 19106, USA

www.jkp.com

Library of Congress Cataloging in Publication Data

Thomas, Mike, 1955-
Fostering a child's recovery : family placement for traumatized children / Mike Thomas and Terry Philpot ; foreword by Mary Walsh.
p. ; cm. -- (Delivering recovery)
Includes bibliographical references and indexes.
ISBN 978-1-84310-327-1 (pb : alk. paper) 1. Abused children--Rehabilitation. 2. Abused children--Services for. 3. Therapeutic foster care. I. Philpot, Terry. II. Title. III. Series.
[DNLM: 1. Child Abuse--therapy. 2. Stress Disorders, Post-Traumatic--therapy. 3. Child. 4. Foster Home Care--psychology. WS 350 T459f 2009]
RJ507.A29T46 2009
362.76'8--dc22

2008037529

British Library Cataloguing in Publication Data
A CIP catalogue record for this book is available from the British Library

ISBN 978 1 84310 327 1

Printed and bound in Great Britain by
Athenaeum Press, Gateshead, Tyne and Wear

To my wife Christine and all our children for their love and inspiration and the many insights they have given me.

Mike Thomas

To Mary for the courage to try and make a difference.

Terry Philpot

A Note and Acknowledgements

This book follows the style of the others in the series whereby a child is referred to as 'she' and adults as 'he' other than in specific cases. However, occasionally, in this book, foster carers have been referred to as 'she' partly because the majority of foster carers are women and in the circumstances it would read strangely to use the male pronoun even when we are writing generally. Names of children and foster carers have been changed.

The authors would like to thank Roger Bullock, a fellow of the Centre for Social Policy, Warren House Group at Dartington, University of Bristol, for turning up some references regarding fostering and residential care and Andrew Hug, then policy officer at Fostering Network, for useful information on fees and allowances. Rebecca Fowler, graduate policy researcher at Barnardo's, supplied statistics that the Department for Children, Families and Schools' website makes peculiarly inaccessible. Ian Sinclair, professor emeritus, York University, elucidated some points about an elusive reference. The SACCS' family placement team provided case examples and Dawn Foulkes showed her forbearance in the face of a mountain of paperwork. As before, Steve Jones, commissioning editor, Jessica Kingsley Publishers, gave help and advice.

Contents

Foreword

In *The World of Children,* Storr (quoted in Buscaglia 1982) writes

> How ignominious to be a child. To be so small that you can be picked
> up, to be moved about at the whim of others. To be fed or not fed. To
> be cleaned or to be left dirty. Made happy or left to cry. It's surely so
> ultimate an indignity that it's not surprising that some of us never
> really recover from it. For it is surely one of the basic fears of
> personkind that we should be treated as things and not as persons.
> Manipulated, pushed around by impersonal forces, treated as of no
> account by the powerful and more superior. Each one of us may be a
> tiny atom in an enormous universe, but we need the illusion that we
> count – that our individuality demands attention. To be able to be
> totally disregarded as a person is a kind of death in life against which
> we have to fight with all our strength.

Children traumatized by serious abuse or profound neglect have suffered
harm to their person, their innocence, their emotional and their spiritual
well-being, and the right to grow up in their own families. Because these
injuries are so profound they affect both their external and internal worlds.
Through no fault of their own they have been injured by one, or both, of
the most important and powerful people in their lives, their parents. For
these children, families are dangerous places where they may be hurt, used
sexually or just ignored, and somehow they think it is their fault. It is not
surprising, therefore, that when placed in another family they will often act
out their beliefs in a frightening and destructive way – both for themselves
and their alternative family – and another rejection will result.

In the next placement the child will test the family even more, and a negative cycle of failed placements begins. Fearful and adrift in the foster care system, every move confirms for the child that the world is a cruel place where you have to fight to survive, and avoid being vulnerable at all costs.

I didn't fully realize the impact of these dynamics until in the early days of SACCS we were visiting children to help them to communicate their distress at what had happened to them. Usually they had been placed with foster carers who had not been trained, prepared or supported in the complex task they had been given. Often the children were still very young, and because of what had happened to them their behaviour was either highly eroticized, or very disturbed. What I saw was carers unable to cope, particularly with the sexualized behaviour and their own sexual feelings about it; the placement broke down and the reason given was always something different. Because the real problem was not identified, the child would be placed in yet another foster home and the same thing happened again and again. The child, re-traumatized by each breakdown, would eventually be placed in residential care – often alongside troubled adolescents who were acting out their own difficulties.

These experiences stayed in my mind when we were creating our integrated therapeutic model of care for children who had had similar experiences. Most of the children who come to us have had multiple moves and serial placement breakdowns. A high proportion of them have had adoption breakdowns, some have poor care plans (if any at all), and often they have incoherent life histories. They are already socially excluded. We have had children placed who have had the wrong name, lost brothers and sisters, and lost parents. Many of them have been more damaged by the system than they were by the original abuse, reinforcing their self-image as untouchable (often literally) and excluded from the mainstream.

In order to redress these issues, it seemed that once they had passed through the recovery programme in our therapeutic residential services, having a positive experience of living in a family was the next piece in helping them to be able to grow up and take their place in society. Families were carefully recruited and assessed for their emotional capacity to do this work, and the resilience to cope with the challenges that would inevitably come. They were trained not just in how to become foster carers, but also in the issues that this group of children bring. Furthermore because we know the children so well, we were able to help the families understand these children's specific needs. The families had access to 24-hour support, and to the knowledge and experience of the children's previous carers. The families are supported to hold the children consistently, so that their recovery could continue and attachments form.

In this book the authors, Mike Thomas and Terry Philpot, share their considerable experience and knowledge on the subject of specialist therapeutic foster care. They explore the history, context and theory of fostering against a backdrop of the complex issues and challenges of looking after children who have been very troubled by their experiences, the dynamics that are at play when a child from one family is transposed into another, and a changing population of children needing care. Add to this new rules and regulations, inspections, and shifting legislation, and it is easy to see the importance of this book in addressing these issues in a practical and practice-focused way. The authors seek to address the issue that love is definitely not enough, and give their readers lots of excellent guidance on how to help placements to succeed. They aim to encourage the carers to be a therapeutic resource for the child, to give them consistency, help them to develop resilience, encourage them in relationships and, in due course, guide them into independence so that they can take their place in society, and bring up their own children safely.

Fostering a Child's Recovery is the fifth and last book in this series about the integrated therapeutic model we have developed at SACCS, and this is apposite since family placement was the last service we offered children as part of their recovery. When a child comes to SACCS they are cared for by a dedicated and well-trained staff who are therapeutic parents to the child during his stay. They use every situation in daily living as a therapeutic opportunity, and look at and explore what is underneath a child's behaviour. The therapeutic team works closely with the therapist and life-story worker, and together as the recovery team they hold the whole child, each part of the work informing the other. About halfway through the child's journey through SACCS, the family placement workers get involved with the recovery team, so that appropriate plans for the child's moving on can be integrated.

A new development at SACCS is a generic fostering service, offering the same standard of nurturing care, for children who have not gone through a therapeutic programme yet need to have a high level of safety input and consistency. This service began last autumn, and we are looking forward to the new challenges and joy that these children will bring with them.

Mary Walsh
Co-founder and Chief Executive of SACCS

Introduction

The origins of fostering reach back to ancient times and, as such, it is, historically, not easy to define. But in the past 30 years fostering has shifted gear, both in terms of the kinds of children and young people with whom it is concerned and also in the gradual professionalization of the service. That said, in terms of the esteem in which it is held and in some other aspects, fostering still lags behind the other professional services with which it engages. Yet it is the most intimate and difficult of all services for children: no one else but the foster carer works with children in their own home, 24 hours a day, seven days a week.

This book, however, is not about family placement generally. It centres upon fostering a certain group of children and young people – those who have been traumatized through sexual and, frequently, physical abuse. Fostering is a valuable and complex task for any kind of child, but we contend that for the children with whom we are concerned the challenges are that much greater, the task that much more complex, and, consequently, the skills required that much more specialized. Such children require more than good parenting or parenting plus – and what that entails, in all its detail, is the central subject of this book, as we describe the fostering process.

However, the interaction between child and carer and carer and the rest of the family placement team has to be set in a wider context. Thus, this book looks at, among other things, the history of fostering and carers and their histories, as well as at the children and what has brought them into the care system.

We also know that within the relationship between child and carer each brings not only their own histories and experiences but also reacts to the impact of fostering itself and its consequences – how do both parties feel about each other? What feelings does fostering evoke in them, especially feelings from their past? But, because the child and the carer are not autonomous and isolated but exist (and should thrive) within the family placement team, we are concerned, too, to look at what those feelings are and how they can be dealt with insofar as they also affect others involved.

Fostering is a stage through which a child and young person passes, even if it can be a long and very difficult one. If fostering is successfully practised the young person, as she comes to adulthood is allowed to make a successful transition to independence. How that is managed is as important as any other part of the process that began when the child first came into the care system. Independence is not a time when the carer says goodbye to the child, any more than a parent says goodbye to his child at the same time in her life. The carer is critical to the young person's transition to independence, and for many carers and young people that relationship continues.

In outlining what good fostering can be (what the nature is of the relationship between carer and child or young person) there are many other issues that we discuss – from recruitment of carers, to the rewards they might expect; from the part played by the carers' own children to the effects of multiple moves on fostered children. But while the child and young person must be the central focus of the whole process – indeed, the central character, so to speak, in this book – our aim has been to show that successful caring for a child must be underpinned by good, effective, supportive and innovative practice for the carer. The one cannot go without the other; the care is dependent on how the carer is supported.

This book is intended to be practical and practice-based but this is set within a context of history, philosophy and theory – all of which can only illuminate, guide and make intelligible good fostering. This book seeks to show that the kind of foster care described here has all the qualities of good parenting but must offer so much more – and what that 'more' is lies at the core of what we describe.

CHAPTER 1

The Context of Family Placement

From myth to modern times: A short history of fostering

The origins of fostering are confused and obscured by the mists of history. Until adoption was legally sanctioned in the UK – in England and Wales in 1926 and in Scotland in 1930 – it was not always easy to discern the different ways in which children who were separated from their families were looked after by others. Certainly, informal adoption – that is, children being taken permanently into the care of a family not headed by its birth parents and treated as a child of that family – has always existed and most societies have devised some kind of arrangement, often with other family members, for children separated from their birth parents.

As in other areas of history that of fostering shows that history is not something that is fixed but rather that it is cyclical – that trends and practices recur or are 're-invented' under new names, often with only slightly different emphases. We now define fostering as a formal arrangement, by local authorities, to place children in substitute family care but without devolving all the legal rights and responsibilities and decision-making that adoptive parents enjoy. However, the past lack of a legal distinction between adoption and fostering and the cultural undertones of how 'family' and its responsibility for children within the extended grouping have been defined in the past makes it difficult to distinguish different kinds of care. But, certainly, children being cared for by other than their birth parents in a family context (as opposed to institutional care) is something attested to by myth and ancient history. For example, the stories of Moses, found abandoned in the bulrushes, and Romulus and Remus, suckled by a she-wolf after being removed from their mother, continue to have a strong cultural resonance. Literature, too, has made use of the orphan, often with dark effect. Novels dealing with this issue range from adult to children's fiction – from Somerset Maugham's *Of Human Bondage* to Philip Pullman's *Ruby in the Smoke*; *The Secret Garden* to *The Cement Garden* and characters from Oliver Twist to Harry Potter, Anne of Green Gables to Jane Eyre. These, together with myth have helped to create a powerful cultural memory that shapes and continues to influence how we think of children who are separated from their birth families.

Before comparatively modern times, there was room for doubt about exactly how to define the living circumstances of such children. For example, Morgan (1998) approvingly quotes Boswell's *The Kindness of Strangers* (1991) when he writes of the care of the ancient world's abandoned children. There was no state intervention to assist them and they might die but they might also be taken in. Boswell says that many households had children 'collected from other families, *who may have been permanent or temporary residents* [our italics], free or servile, legally adopted or simply supported'. So while Boswell tells us that there was a form of legal adoption and that children could be 'temporary or permanent residents', we could assume this is what we now think of as fostering, even if Moses' and Oedipus' case notes are not available for inspection! Indeed, the mixing of informal adoption and fostering in the distant past has its modern equivalent whereby the definitional differences between long-term fostering and adoption are not always easy to sustain, other than in a legal sense.

Fostering could be found in Ireland in medieval times and, in the absence of any legal basis for fostering, all 'fostering' that occurred then can be taken as having been private fostering.[1] There are even references to private fostering much earlier than the celebrated and notorious case of Mrs Waters and her 'baby farm' in 1870. (She was tried and executed for the murder of several foster children.) It was as a result of this case, as Holman (1973) has shown, that, in 1872, the Protection of Infant Life Act came onto the statute books – the first recognition by the state of its duty in this area.

Before then records show young orphans being placed with nurses in the London suburbs at a time when institutional care was the norm. These children were very probably in monastic or private institutions, as the workhouse – a state institution – did not come into being until the Poor Law Act 1601. Wet nurses, who originated in France around 1450, can be seen as foster carers in an important contemporary sense (Triseliotis, Sellick and Short 1995b). They were paid for by the state and expected to keep the children up to the age of 12. Many children, it is believed, were absorbed within the nurses' own families as a form of *de facto* adoption. The wet-nurse system was adopted in England and Scotland by the foundling hospitals in London and Glasgow but, unlike in France, the children went back to their families or institutions when they were five or six. Later the children would be put out as apprentices.

The first instance of recognizably professional fostering in modern times is probably that instituted by the Foundling Hospital (later the Thomas Coram Foundation and now Coram Family) in London. It is the country's oldest children's charity, created in 1739 and opened in 1741. From the very beginning babies were boarded out – that is, fostered – in their first five years with wet nurses. They were then brought back to live at the hospital. Medicine had, by then, recognized that babies should be breastfed rather than have a diet of dried crusts and chicken. The hospital's wet nurses were subject to initial selection procedures, given advice on child care and inspected by either the matron or the steward of the hospital, and there were later local inspections. In 1853 Dickens visited the hospital and recorded that the wet nurses were paid six pence (2½ p) a day and 14 shillings (70p) a year for babies, and 18 shillings (90p) for four- and five-year-olds (Pugh 2007). It is safe to assume that payment of fees and allowances had been made to wet nurses before this time.

In 1818 the policy of calling the children back to their families of origin was abandoned in Glasgow when it was decided to encourage the children to be brought up by families with whom they were originally placed until they found their way in life. This is the system which, in the UK, collapsed in the wake of the baby farming scandals and the consequent legislation mentioned above. Ruegger and Rayfield (1999) date modern fostering – that is, payment to the carer with statutory oversight – to the Reverend Armistead in 1853 in Cheshire, who placed children from a workhouse with foster parents. The local authority was legally responsible for them and paid the foster parents an allowance equivalent to the cost of maintaining them in the workhouse. A few years later, the authors go on to say, a Mrs Hannah Archer in Swindon placed a number of orphaned girls with foster carers. They were paid the basic workhouse allowance and a supplement of voluntary contributions.

Although there was initial opposition to fostering – it was believed it would encourage feckless and irresponsible parents on the one hand or money-grasping exploitive carers on the other – its practice grew. To some extent, at least with regard to ambivalence about people being paid to look after other people's children, this is echoed in the modern popular misunderstandings about the professionalization of fostering. But the belief that children ought to have some kind of substitute family care was encouraged by pioneering philanthropists like Thomas Barnardo and Thomas Bowman Stephenson, founder of the National Children's Home & Orphanage (now Action for Children), with their reaction against children being cared for in large institutions. In the 1860s the National Committee for the Boarding Out of Pauper Children was concerned not only with the damaging effects of institutional care but also saw boarding out as a means by which girls – the committee consisted of women – could be trained and thus would be created a larger supply of labour, particularly for domestic service (Philpot 1994).[2]

A third of all Barnardos' children were in foster care by 1891 (Parker 1990) and while the National Children's Home did not mention boarding out in its annual reports until 1908 it said this had been going on since the 1880s. By 1909 a quarter of the Home's children were cared for in this way (Philpot 1994). But those responsible for running the workhouses were also charged with boarding out some of the children living there. There were 98 such officials in 1908, only six of whom had specific responsibility for placements, and until 1911 only abandoned or orphaned children aged between 2 and 10 could be boarded out. (Today local authority practice guidance tends to suggest that no child under 12 should be in residential care.) It was only gradually over the past 25 to 30 years that children and young people with a learning difficulty, those who were physically disabled, those in trouble with the law, and those with difficult personalities came to be seen as being able to be fostered.

Barnardo and Stephenson, with some others, also engaged in an experiment in mass fostering. Children had first been migrated to Canada by philanthropists Maria Rye in 1868 and Annie MacPherson in 1869. Stephenson brought the big battalions of the children's charities to the endeavour when the National Children's Home first sent children to Canada in 1873 and Barnardo followed in 1882. There were varying motives for this new direction. It was partly to replenish the white Protestant stock of the colonies but there was also a belief that the cities were places of vice and temptation and that taking children away from this was to make a surgical cut in their existences, create a new life and a new start. The new land had, believed Stephenson, 'a moral tone', the strong influence of religion and plentiful work. The concept of 'rescue', embodied in the names of children's societies, especially Catholic ones, was a strong one, underwritten by the moral concept. Indeed, 'moral' was a term often found at this time – as in children being in 'moral danger' – as well as much later when moral welfare associations flourished in the late 19th and early 20th centuries. Indeed, the Association of Moral Welfare Workers was only wound up in 1975 (Wagner 1982).

Particularly in the idea of rescue, there are echoes of the anti-urbanism of William Morris and the work of the garden city pioneers (Philpot 1994). Urban living was seen as being unhealthy and dangerous, hence the retreat to the country and new forms of idealized living. For the child-care pioneers, urban living meant exposing the children to all kinds of temptation and depravity, hence their export to the healthy, open spaces of the colonies. These children were often boarded as hands with far-flung farming families, who would have taken them in as some approximation of a family member rather than merely another worker. The National Children's Home, in particular, did inspect the placements and attempt to monitor them, although given distances and communications, this was probably more easily intended than done. Other charities followed – Fairbridge Farm Schools and some of the Catholic charities among them – and children began to be sent to New Zealand and Australia. The National Children's Home were still sending children to Canada in the 1950s, while Barnardo's persisted until the 1960s (Wagner 1982).

The mass evacuation during World War II when children were taken away from the cities, which were the targets of bombing raids, to live with families in the country was another example of fostering on a mass scale (or 'boarding out' as it was still called and would be for some time to come). This policy was to have far-reaching personal and political consequences (see especially Holman 1995). The personal consequences were felt by the children, some of whom had suffered greatly, physically and emotionally, at being separated from their parents. But the death of one child, Denis O'Neill, in January 1945, who had been boarded out by his local authority, gave particular impetus to public concern. O'Neill's death was a precursor of the child abuse cases that came to public attention in the 1970s and continue to the present day. It was not until the death of Maria Colwell, at the hands of her stepfather in 1974, that public, media and political attention would again be unremittingly directed on children who die at the hands of parents, step-parents and, occasionally, other relatives but the O'Neill case was notable in that the perpetrator was a foster carer and significant in that it led to radical reforms.

The government had already announced at the end of 1944 that it would set up a committee to consider 'the existing methods of providing for children deprived of a normal home life'. (This was the wording of the terms of reference for the Curtis Committee.) This had come as a result of agitation by Lady Allen of Hurtwood and grew also from what evacuation was revealing to the receiving families about the kind of public (which also meant charitable) care from which many of the children came. O'Neill's savage death – he was beaten and starved – prompted the setting up of the Curtis Committee in 1946. The Committee recommended the creation of children's departments, which were then created by the Children Act 1948. But often forgotten is the report's stipulation that all children in care should be fostered unless this was 'not practicable or desirable for the time being'. The Act also formalized the assessment and selection of foster parents, guidelines for which had, in fact, existed under the Poor Law. But change after that was slow: indeed, until fairly recently the Boarding-Out Regulations of 1955 still governed much of fostering. The regulations were updated in 1988 and absorbed, with minor alteration, in the Children Act 1989, and we now have the Fostering Services Regulations 2002.

With Curtis' recommendations and philosophy accepted, two factors now came into play. First, Curtis had given a great boost to boarding out but, second, a growing general distrust of residential provision for children began to develop, from which the sector has never really recovered. This has contributed to the later radical turning away from residential care. These two matters were to affect markedly the pattern of children's services and to lead eventually, among other things, to the realization that children with certain disabilities and other characteristics thought to weigh against them, could be either fostered or adopted.

The 1960s might be judged the liberal hour when it came to the care of children and young people. There were progressive reports like that by the committee headed by Lord Longford (1964), the White Papers, *The Child, The Family and the Young Offender* (Home Office 1965) and *Children in Trouble* (Home Office 1968), and the passing of the Children and Young Persons Act 1963. These aimed to reduce the number of children and young people coming into care and were part of a reforming tide which, with the passing of the Children and Young Persons Act 1969, was to sweep away approved schools. There was agitation for a family-based service and an end to the dichotomy of children as being regarded 'deprived or depraved'. This led to the Seebohm Report (Committee on Local Authority and Allied Personal Social Services 1970), which, in turn, led to the Local Authority Social Services Act 1968, which abolished the children's departments and created the all-embracing social services departments.

These departments were to last 30 years until, more by government fiat than any thought-through recommendations resulting from a committee, they were replaced by separated children's services departments and adults services departments. However, the children's services departments were more than the old children's department reborn because these were geared to regard children within their areas holistically and as a result the education departments were also brought under their roof. However, not all local authorities adapted this approach and, at the time of writing, some have in fact re-formed their services to create family services departments more like the former social services departments.

But so far as fostering was concerned 30 years ago, it continued to be influenced by thinking that was pointing away from institutional care to a more permanent family life for children. This is evidenced, in particular, in the work of John Bowlby (1973–1980) and Rowe and Lambert (1973). Bowlby drew attention to the importance of a child's attachment to a 'primary carer' if she was to have a satisfactory emotional development.

Rowe and Lambert's *Children who Wait* (1973) drew attention to the tendency of children to go into care and drift without any plan for alternative, community-based placement or rehabilitation within their birth family. What children required, they argued, was a strong sense of belonging to a family.

This was welcome news for children languishing in care, but, as Thoburn (1999) has written, 'the cracks in the foster care service began to appear and permanence policies emerged'. There was a strong emphasis still in legislation to allow adoption without parental consent and 'permanent family care generally equated with adoption'. (McAndrew 2000). Foster care, then, was intended either to help unite children with their birth families or to prepare them for adoption. There was, as McAndrew also says, a 'backlash against the idea of long-term foster care as a placement of choice'. The change in terminology – from foster parent to foster carer – recognized this. That changed title also reflects the idea that fostering is essentially about caring and that one of the tasks of the foster carer is to act like a good parent but also, for many children, to offer something more. Thus, the concept of what foster care is has widened.

But while fostering continued even those who favoured it often still saw it as naturally the preserve of women and something that, because 'natural', did not require special training. This attitude was one that for too long helped both to shape the service and to characterize it in the public eye: the foster carer was a woman who exhibited common sense and homely virtues. (This was a concept unhelpfully and eccentrically revived in the 1990s when the then Secretary of State for Health, Virginia Bottomley, said that social workers needed to be 'street-wise grannies'.) Foster carers still require common sense and homely virtues but they also require much more (and always did) for what is a highly demanding job. This had been recognized with the development in Kent in the 1970s of a 'professional' fostering service for adolescents (Hazel 1981). And so it was that in 1984 the Short Report (House of Commons Social Services Committee 1984), some of whose major recommendations were to be realized in the Children Act 1989, could state:

> Side by side with the growth of foster care in general has been the development of specialist or "professional" fostering where the added difficulty of some foster parents' task is recognised by additional

payment, and of fostering by parents who some years ago would have been considered unsuitable.

However, ideas of a fresh start and severing family links for children in favour of permanent solutions began to be questioned and short-term fostering began to be seen as something that had much to offer children. The Children Act 1989 was concerned to offer a service for families rather than deprive them of their children, and in this fostering had an obvious part to play. Partnership with parents, contact, accommodation as a part of family support, parents retaining parental responsibility even when children were in care, the no order principle,[3] and, above all, the 'paramouncy' of the best interests of the child – all of these marked the new legislation as a fresh approach in the way that birth families, family support and the needs of children were seen.

But while a professional view that regarded fostering as the hand-maiden of permanency weakened considerably, adoption came to have a second wind. The local authority circular of 1998, *Adoption: Achieving the Right Balance*, aimed to correct some of the faults in getting children adopted and bring it back into the mainstream of professional social-work endeavour; while Tony Blair's personal interest in adoption, as prime minister, revived some of the arguments of Rowe and Lambert (1973) about children being lost in care. This culminated in the Adoption and Children Act 2002, by which it was intended to speed up the adoption process and to help more children to be adopted.

But fostering is a very different creature from what it was even only 15 or 20 years ago. This is evidenced in the rise of the independent agency (Sellick 1999; Sellick and Connolly 2001), the growing professionalism of the service, the characteristics of the children now to be found in care and in need of fostering, and the widening group of children believed to be fosterable. All of this and the wish to meet the needs of families and children, has meant that a wide variety of fostering has been developed: emergency, long-term, short-term, intermediate, remand, concurrent (Gray 2002), and therapeutic, as well as the gathering interest in kinship care (Broad 2001) (see later in this chapter). However, while the even wider variety of children now thought able to be fostered and these varied forms of foster care have been developed, it is arguable that residential care has been downplayed. Despite local authority practice guidance on children under 12 not being in residential care, some children require residential care of a very specialized nature before they can go into fostering because of the severity of the abuse which they have suffered. This we know but it is almost as if our understanding has outstripped the kinds of provision we think suitable.

Foster carers themselves have changed – the majority remain married couples but single and gay people also foster; foster carers are sometimes seen as part of a professional multi-disciplinary team and they are not merely trained but can obtain a National Vocational Qualification, as well as The Bridge's Diploma in Therapeutic Fostering and SACCS' Foundation Degree in Therapeutic Child Care. In England their representation on the Children's Workforce Development Council was seen as recognition of their professional status. Fostering has also been influenced by initiatives like Quality Protects, Sure Start, efforts to prevent social exclusion, and the introduction of legislation like the Children (Leaving Care) Act 2000 (which was occasioned partly by the low level of educational achievement attained by young people leaving care and the lack of support for them when they do so). However, the concerns about looked-after children and, in particular, their educational attainment led to the publication, in 2006 of the Green Paper, *Care Matters* (Department for Education and Skills 2006), and, the Children and Young Persons Act, which passed into law as this book went to press.

There have also been performance indicators introduced for local authorities to reduce the number of moves to three a year which children make in care and, thus, to afford them greater stability. However, even if these indicators are adhered to (and all the evidence shows that many children's departments are not attaining them), a young person who came into care at six could by the age of 18 still have had 36 placements – and even half that number is half too many. Fostering has also been affected by the recognition that children and young people have rights and not the least of these is to have their opinions taken into account.

However, despite all these changes and the fact that fostering is the mostly widely used form of care for children living away from their families, it is not a priority among local authorities or the Department for Children, Schools and Families, it gets very little media attention, and is rarely a matter that politicians take up. There are 60,000 children and young people in care in England, yet the 42,300 (72 per cent) children living in foster care and the 3,300 children who are adopted from care receive attention in inverse proportion to their numbers (Department for Children, Schools and Families 2008).

In March 2002 the government announced a major review of fostering and placement in the wake of a damning report on fostering services from the Social Services Inspectorate (Department for Health 2002a). This was followed in 2006 with the Green Paper, *Care Matters* (Department for Education and Skills 2006). This, it was hoped, would take give fostering the serious attention hitherto frequently denied it. Fostering needs to be regarded as a critical service for children and young people; there needs to be a change from the current situation in which intimate daily caring is set against a backdrop of inconsistent rewards for carers, their uncertain status, and the chronic problem of recruiting them. What fostering is in reality; the paramount role it plays in the lives of tens of thousands of children and young people; how good practice can be enhanced; and what fostering requires to move forward and so be accorded worth, status, value and recognition – to describe each of these is the purpose of the rest of this book.

Questions

- What does history tell us about fostering?

- Is fostering seen as a panacea?

- Give two examples of the ways in which the history of fostering or children's services have generally repeated themselves?

- Why do you think that inverse attention is given to the comparatively small number of children adopted each year against the large number who are in foster care?

Kinship care: keeping it in the family

Kinship care – when children in care (or on the edge of care) are looked after by family or friends with the agreement of children's services departments – is nothing new, even though the ordinary observer might be led to believe otherwise with the interest in it over the past few years. Guidance accompanying the Children Act 1989, the Children (Scotland) Act 1995 and the Children (Northern Ireland) Order 1995 all stated that local authorities should explore placing children with their relatives or family friends before looking to foster care with someone unknown to the child. In 1998 the National Foster Care Association issued a policy statement giving full support to kinship care as a preferred option (National Foster Care Association 1998). But kinship care can be dated even further back. Research goes back to at least 1982 (Lahti 1982) and, according to Holman (2002), in 1958 Manchester children's department had 44 per cent of its children in care fostered by relatives as opposed to 21 per cent of the then national average.

And yet more than a decade after the Children Act 1989 studies (Broad 2001; Broad, Hayes and Rushforth 2001) had characterized kinship care as 'largely invisible as a policy issue', around which, the second group of authors added, 'there is a dearth of information and much confusion surrounding its definition' (Broad *et al.* 2001).

However, it is not just that this kind of care has only comparatively recently started to creep very slowly into professional thinking. Fostered children in the UK are looked after markedly differently from their counterparts in other Western countries. Eleven per cent (7,000) of children of all looked-after children in England were in a foster placement with a relative or friend in the year ending 31 March 2007 (Department for Children, Schools and Families 2008). At the other end of the scale is Poland with 90 per cent of its looked-after children so cared for, followed by New Zealand with 75 per cent. The USA and Belgium both have a third of looked-after children (33 per cent) cared for by family and friends, while Sweden looks after 25 per cent of its children in care in this way (Greeff 1999). But even the UK's 11 per cent hides glaring inconsistencies because 'historically' returns show that within individual local authorities they range from nil to 20 per cent. Within the UK there are differences from country and to country. For example, in Wales in 2000 nearly a fifth of fostered children live with a relative (Welsh Assembly 2001), although by 2007 the percentage was the same as that for England (BAAF 2008). However, in Scotland the percentage was 15 per cent in 2007 (Scottish

Assembly 2007) and in Northern Ireland nearly 20 per cent (19.9 per cent) (Department of Health, Social Services and Public Safety 2007).

Research suggests that kinship placements had more stability than other kinds of placement – Broad *et al.* (2001) found that nearly half (46 per cent) had lasted continuously for between one and five years and a third for over five years. But the administrative categories through which the placements were made differed greatly – some were under section 17 of the Children Act 1989, others were residence or care orders.

Broad *et al* (2001) also reflect some of the findings of Wheal and Waldeman (1999). In the latter study, 38 per cent of kinship carers were grandparents, a quarter were aunts and 14 per cent were friends. And, again, children from ethnic minorities were over-represented in this kind of care: 31 per cent were of Guyanese and Caribbean origin; 27 per cent were English, Welsh or Scottish and 31 per cent were of mixed race.

How do the children regard kinship care? Wheal and Waldeman (1999) reported that children's reactions depended on prior relationships with the carers and the age of the children, while the presence of siblings eased separation anxieties (kinship cared-for children are more likely to be cared for with their brothers and sisters than other looked-after children); and it also depended on the situation in which they were living.

Broad *et al.* (2001) quote one young person who spoke graphically of their feelings about their care and who, perhaps, summed up the general feelings:

> I love to know that I belong to somebody, I'm loved by people and it's good to know that I have got somewhere to come after school that I can call home.

These young people generally expressed what the authors refer to as 'emotional permanence' – feeling safe and secure living with their extended family – which came from the love that they received.

Young people also refer to the other advantages of being fostered by relatives:

- stability
- avoiding local authority care and being looked after by strangers
- feeling safe from adults

- maintaining links with family, brothers and sisters and friends

- sustaining their racial and cultural heritage; and

- being supported in their education.

Another researcher (Kosensen 1993) found, in a study in Scotland, that children in the care of their relatives were more likely to return to their families.

Five other research studies – two of them in the USA – have all come to the same conclusion about the success of placing the full range of children with relatives as opposed to those whom they do not know (Barth, Courtney, Berrick and Albert 1994; Berridge and Cleaver 1987; Fein, Maluccio, Hamilton and Ward 1983; Lahti 1982; Rowe, Hundleby and Keane 1984). They compared children from similar backgrounds on a range of measures. Relatives, they conclude, according to a summary by Sellick, Thoburn and Philpot (2004):

> have a particular advantage of being able to help the child with identity issues at the same time as providing a higher level of care than was available than when the child was living with the birth parents. (p.68)

However, these writers go on to warn:

> placement with relatives is becoming a placement of choice in a wider range of circumstances in the UK and in America, and it may be that more risks will be taken and consequently the proportion of successful placements will decrease. (p.68)

Broad *et al.* (2001) also saw disadvantages placing children with relatives in terms of limitations on the children and young people's freedom, financial hardship, and the inability to gain access to care leavers' services.

A myth has grown up, among public and politicians, about children in care which says that they are separated irretrievably from their parents. This may have something to do with lingering, residual notions of 'abandonment' and 'orphans' but it may also be to do with the widespread but wholly mistaken belief that the answer to the problem of children in care is that they should be adopted. This has been, after all, the motivating force and clear implication of the government's reforms in the Adoption and Children Act 2002. Nonetheless, the majority of looked-after children in the UK are in foster care, a majority return to their families and while subject to a care order a significant minority of children and young people continue to live at home.

That their birth family is important to care leavers is well attested to in research (Marsh and Peel 1999). Their main attachments are to mothers, grandparents, aunts and brothers and sisters rather than fathers. Care leavers from ethnic minorities have been found to have fewer family contacts than white care leavers have, which makes kinship care all the more attractive as a care alternative.

There is also the preventative aspect of kinship care. Richards (2001) shows that children who are cared for by their grandparents, whose parents may have abused them and/or have a mental illness or are substance misusers, would otherwise go into local authority care.

Yet children's expressed attachment to their family and friends is not one that is generally heeded by social workers. A study for the Department of Health found that the majority of care leavers could name a relative whom they felt they could rely on and the nominated family member could confirm this. But they also found that in the majority of cases the young person's social worker had no idea who this so-called 'key kin' was and that person had not been invited to the reviews (Marsh and Peel 1999). Social workers may well regard any such relative as unsafe or not competent, and believe that a child in their care won't be protected. They may also think a grandparent is not the right person with whom to place the child when she or he has raised the parent who has "failed".

So, difficult though it is to recruit foster carers generally, finding kinship carers does not appear to be a priority for most local authorities – even though this kind of care does appear to have certain advantages. However, as well as listening to what children say there are some other methods of finding family and friends carers that have proven successful. Family group conferences can be made use of – as has been done in other countries and is being done more and more in the UK. These conferences have been instrumental in 'discovering' family and friends willing to be involved in the care of looked-after children. Some of the 'discovered' friends and relatives were previously unknown to social services and had not been involved in the child's plans before; some had had previous involvement and had chosen not to be involved with social services; or they had been discouraged by the low level of support offered to them. Some of these friends and relatives became kinship carers and it is not impossible that other children (either living with strangers or in residential care), could benefit from care by kin if the group-conference method were used to find such carers. However, if family group conferences are to play a significant role in finding kinship carers, they will need to be more widely used by local authorities – at the moment only a minority of local authorities in England and Wales make use of them.

As McGill (2003) has pointed out, the undervaluing of kinship care is not merely one of attitude. In practical terms, he says, the difference in the treatment of foster carers and kinship carers is 'considerable'. At the time McGill was writing, a foster carer could receive as much as £250 a week allowance and have the support of two named social workers (one for the child and one for the carers), whereas a kinship carer might receive up to £80 and have one named social worker (for the child) or no specific support service. He even offers as an example of the invisibility of kinship care the fact that anyone approaching what was then a social services department and asking to be put in touch with teams working with kinship carers, family and friends carers or residence order carers[4] was likely to be disappointed – they don't exist.

There is a danger that local authorities may assume that kinship carers do not need the support and training that other foster carers expect and receive because this kind of care is 'natural' – and some kinship carers may also feel this. After all, they have not been recruited to care for other people's children; they are caring for children in their own family, using what they may feel were the proven techniques they applied to their own children when small. Does this mean that they may resent the idea that they need training? Perhaps so, but research has indicated that kinship carers feel as much in need of training and support as anyone else. What the local authority or agency needs to stress is what it expects of kinship carers, just as it does of stranger foster carers. Unless they do this, local authorities may end up treating kinship carers as they did foster carers 25 years ago.

However, situations when kinship should be queried (which is not to say dismissed) do exist, and these are where children have suffered abuse at the hands of a family member. Hunt, Waterhouse and Lutman (2008) found that while kinship care can be a positive option for many abused and neglected children, it is not straightforward and requires careful assessment and adequate support. Clearly, there are questions to be asked in these cases. For example, if the child is to be placed with a grandparent and that person is the father or mother of the offender what do we know of their parenting skills? What happens if the child discloses past abuse for the first time or current or further abuse by a family member – how will the kinship carer deal with disclosure about someone to whom they may be close? It is important that, in all circumstances, the dynamics of child abuse are not lost and that the safety of the child is always paramount. This may well need to include physical and emotional distance from the family. These are questions and considerations that all need to be raised and which may prove that, in some cases, kinship care is not suitable for a child traumatized through abuse.

So while kinship care is not unproblematic, it is an option that is only slowly being more widely discovered, and that needs to be encouraged. It has distinct advantages, the major one being that children are cared for by people whom they know and are not separated from their families. Placements are also far less likely to be transracial because there are disproportionately more kinship carers from ethnic minorities groups than there are among stranger foster carers.

Although there has been an increasing interest in kinship care in England it was Scotland that launched a national strategy for kinship care in 2006 (Fostering Network, 2007). Under this, approved kinship carers (those caring for a looked-after or accommodated child) will have access to the same level of financial and practical support as non-related foster carers (including receiving the same allowances). The Scottish Executive has also allocated money to the Citizen's Advice Bureaux to help ensure that those on foster care payments receive the state benefits to which they are entitled.

Additional questions about kinship care for traumatized children are raised by those who apply to be foster carers not only during their assessment phase, but also in their practice as a carer, as they recognise their caring is more than just that for a family member. Traumatized children frequently have specific needs, and specific parenting needs beyond the norm – what Maginn (2006) call the 'pillars of parenting' and Schofield and Beek (2006a) refer to as 'mind-mindedness' (keeping the child in mind) after the work of Miens (1997). Can kinship carers adapt to these new demands and move beyond what is traditional and now act as therapeutic carers? The key to success for the kinship care of traumatized children will be in accepting and working with both aspects of the placement – that of the kin and family and the role of the carer working in a specified way. This latter aspect is difficult for all. It requires kinship carers to embrace the role of the foster carers, as people working in the whole system, with responsibilities to others, and also to accept that fostering in this way is more than just looking after children (i.e. what they did for their own children) but is actually a job with professional responsibilities.

Kinship carers should not be accepted simply because they are family and friends. The care they can offer and the environment, physical and otherwise, in which the child would live may well be inferior to that which a foster carer who is unrelated to the child could offer. But that is a matter of assessment for the local authority. Kinship care is not a cost-free option for children's services but it is a resource that is still often overlooked at a time when more resources are posited as the main answer to most of social care's problems.

Questions

- What are the arguments that influence whether a kinship placement is beneficial to a child who has been traumatized?

- What benefits might kinship care have over care by someone unknown to the child and what might be the disadvantages?

- If you were to become a kinship carer, how might this affect your wider family?

Art, not science

Foster care, like all aspects of social care, is (quite rightly) governed and regulated by legislation, guidance, rules and regulations. In recent years these have increased in volume (as is the case with other areas) and the stated aim is the welfare and protection of children who are taken into foster care. However, foster care is about a relationship between carer and child. Like all human relationships it is determined and governed by matters far more powerful than rules and regulations: interaction between the parties, reaction to each other, personal histories, an understanding why both are now living together (which may not be a shared understanding), warmth, enjoyment, resentment, anger, loss, uncertainty – and a whole range of other reactions and emotions.

Fostering, then, is about how both carer and child *feel* – about each other and about the circumstances in which they find themselves. At the heart of relationships are feelings and their impact on us. Furthermore, a child's feelings may be based not only on her reaction to the carer and her situation but also to the physical environment in which she finds herself – what she sees, touches and smells. What does that smell, that sight or that texture conjure up for her? What does it remind her of? Is it a positive or negative recollection? Even the most everyday matters – the smell of perfume, a certain hairstyle, the way a meal is set on the table, or the style in which a room is painted or furnished – these may be critical to how the child reacts to her new home and the person who is caring for her and others in the household.

The foster carer is someone who does not work by a rule book but who employs imaginative skill in the relationship with the child. It is the interplay between imagination and feelings that influences the outcome of fostering. Imaginative skill is a cornerstone of art and so, we would argue, fostering is much more of an art than a science. The cornerstone of fostering is the relationship between carers and the child and her interaction with the wider world. The reasons behind positive outcomes are often not easy to quantify. The factors that make one placement work and another fail can be hard to identify because of the myriad interactions between foster carer and child.

The relationship between two people is unique: no matter how similar this foster carer may seem to another or this child to another, each will act differently when matched with the other. Likewise, the family into which each child goes is different and those assessing foster carers need to look at how families are organized: the relationships between members, how they eat at meal times, how they react to pressure, and so on. These are far more significant for the appropriate matching of child to carer and the outcome of the placement than the more standard and usual assessments of what the family's interests are or the state of the home. It is often those matters that lie outside the rules, regulations and formal processes that hold the key to success.

Much fostering research (Farmer, Moyers and Lipscombe 2004; Sinclair 2005) has concentrated on the aspects of what makes fostering work by looking at factors frequently present when placements fail. It is now a truism that placements need to avoid being made where there are children of similar ages or children who are within two, three or five years of one another (depending on what research is read). But are we talking about chronological age or developmental or emotional age, and how do we assess these ages? Equally, how do we explain that not all similar age placements disrupt? What makes those that endure successful? It would seem to us that this offers a rich vein of further research.

Our contention is that success will relate to the parenting style and understanding of the carer and the openness of the child to receiving the care. For traumatized children, many of whom will have an attachment disorder, it will be the feelings evoked for the carer and how these are managed that will decide whether or not a placement will last. It is this emotional regulation that we need to look at.

The more foster care seeks to be scientific and to be based upon rules and competencies, the more this understanding of the extra dimension of fostering is lost. If this happens in the fostering of traumatized children then we do these children a disservice by placing them in families, because without this dimension we lack a full understanding of children, of the effect of trauma on people, and of the capacity of traumatized children to recreate circumstances of breakdown with which they are familiar (Tomlinson 2008).

Questions

- How do feelings affect placement?

- Where do those feelings come from?

- Whose feelings are they?

- Why do placements work, as opposed to why they do not?

- Think of four things in the relationship between foster carer and child that are similar to those in the relationship between child and birth parent, and four things which are different between the two relationships. How do each of these affect feelings?

What does fostering offer?

There is a contradiction at the heart of fostering. It is an attempt to offer substitute family care for children who have been removed from families where they have been harmed. It can be, therefore, an attempt to offer them something that the child is fearful of because it has been damaging in the past. There are, of course, some children and young people who actively resist fostering and adoption and state their preference for residential care. Barry (2001), in a Scottish study, found that young people:

> voiced graver concerns about foster care than they did about residential care, suggesting that the latter provided for a more secure, safer and longer-term environment for young people in need of care. (p.30)

Barry admits that this ran contrary to the conventional wisdom, which preferred foster care to residential care. She said that there were two reasons why young people felt as they did.

- First, residential placements were more likely to offer greater scope for long-term stability and, therefore, consistency of care.

- Second, the young people did not see foster care as necessarily an appropriate alternative to their own families and 'they resented the often poor replication of "family life"' (p.30). Some children cannot manage the pressure of being seen as somebody else's child, and, indeed, do not want that intimacy.

Kahan (1979) and Berridge (1985) took the view that most *teenagers* preferred residential care, although Hudson and Galloway (1989) and Hazel's work (1981) showed that even the most difficult teenagers *can* be fostered (see Chapter 3). Triseliotis and colleagues (1995a) say that teenagers and birth parents are equally divided in their preferences for foster care and residential care.

Aldgate (1989) makes a comparison, within the context of permanency planning, where the birth family will be the preferred source of permanence in most cases. She argues that foster care has a great deal to offer many children and is undoubtedly preferable for young children. However, she goes on to say that residential care is a genuine and important alternative for some older children.

In a major study of children's homes, Sinclair and Gibbs (1998a) interviewed 223 children in residential care. The results were roughly that a third had not wished to enter care, a third had mixed feelings about this and a third were in favour of it. Given that they were in care, they were much more likely to prefer residential care to foster care (Sinclair and Gibbs 1998b, p.79). However, the only children studied were those in residential care and not those in foster care. The children's negative responses to foster care may have been conditioned by the fact that they felt insecure and feared change. It would not mean that the preferred option was necessarily good for them. Also, some of the more difficult young people might prefer foster care for the wrong reasons: therapeutically, they might need to be challenged or encouraged to develop emotionally, whereas stays in residential care may prevent this by allowing them to continue in an undemanding environment. This might be good or bad for them, depending on the individual (Bullock 2008). There may be other reasons, too, why young people in care should feel this way. It may be because of the trauma that the young person has suffered; or it may be that the many moves which she has endured cause her to want the stability that residential care seemingly offers.

Fostering may also not be the best placement for children who have been severely abused. For them, residential care in a therapeutic environment will be best suited to their needs, with the ultimate goal being to find them a substitute family. Thus, while the wishes and needs of children and young people have to be respected, fostering remains the chosen option for most children in care who are separated from their families and the ultimate placement for those who will have required therapy.

With very few exceptions, all societies are based on the family unit, nuclear or extended. Even family breakup is usually caused by the wish to create a new family. Young people in care may do as the majority do and will one day form their own families. Their re-introduction to family life, through fostering, offers them not only stability and the care available from their foster carers but also a familiarization with the way in which healthy families can function. Residential care can only offer so much responsibility or opportunity to experiment, and it is also necessarily regimented, with set times for activities, and so on. Those who live in residential situations can be required to conform much more to the wishes of others with whom they are placed and the needs of others, and can be much more subject to formalities than are those in live-in families. A good foster family, on the other hand, can offer children and young people the chance to take some control over their lives, to accept responsibility, to give as well as to take in the daily round of family life. This is important for all children and young people but especially so for those who are looked-after and who are in residential care because this social learning will have been disrupted – either by entry into residential care or because it may not have been easily acquired in the kind of families from which they came. A foster family allows such children to acquire and practise everyday social skills in a normal setting.

According to the Social Care Institute for Excellence (2004) successful fostering includes:

- A parenting style which combines boundaries with warmth.

- An expectation that the relationship with the child will survive.

- An emphasis on the relationship and on flexible problem solving within it.

- Facilitating contact with birth parents and avoiding criticism.

- Flexibility and not being easily upset.

- Encouragement about education and school.

Other research (Borland, O'Hara and Triseliotis 1991; Sinclair, Gibbs and Wilson 2004) has said that carers need to be:

- clear, firm, and able to combine warmth and understanding with guidance and control

- child orientated

- warm and responsive

- flexible and not easily upset

- tolerant and able to carry on; and

- able to handle disturbed attachment behaviour.

The way to recovery

The recovery process is about making progress and recognizing changes in oneself and in the environment. The work of SACCS is enabling each child on the process of recovery to achieve the recovery outcomes as set out (Tomlinson and Philpot). If we take only eight of the outcomes for the purposes of illustration, we can see how the process of day-to-day living can be readily applied to them when the child has to be able to:

- show appropriate reactions
- develop internal controls
- make the best use of opportunities
- make appropriate choices
- make appropriate relationships with adults or those of her own age
- take responsibility
- develop insight; and
- develop motor skills (Pughe and Philpot 2007, pp.113–118).

Thus, family placement is offered so that there is an opportunity for the outcomes the child has met in residential care to be transferred to other situations.

Children and young people learn better how these outcomes can be achieved through living in a family because they are more easily experienced there, but, in doing that, they also learn how to apply them to a variety of settings. Learning to be patient when forced to wait for service in a pub has an application far wider than simply wanting to order cannelloni! It is about self-regulation, self-discipline and internalizing boundaries. Practical tasks and experiences – when to take food from the table, whether to offer a drink to someone else – are also social experiences that allow us to learn how to relate to others. This is something we learn in these day-to-day transactions in family life.

The SACCS outcomes, then, are not checklists for children and young people to learn but actions and reactions which they internalize (as we all do) and eventually come to practise naturally and spontaneously.

Fahlberg (2003) says that one of the functions of family:

> is to provide continuous contact with a small number of people over a lifetime. The long-term relationships between family members allow each person an opportunity to clarify past events and reinterpret past events in terms of the present. Children in care are frequently denied these opportunities. They change families; they change workers; they may lose contact with birth family members.

Foster care can offer children separated from their birth families the opportunity of having a family life, within a substitute family – to experience and re-experience it, this time positively.

For traumatized children, fostering offers all of the above, but it is also situated in the family, an inherently frightening place – a place where trauma has been experienced previously. Many of these children, therefore, react against families and view them as not being places to which they want to return (which may account for the findings of Barry (2001) already quoted).

In placing traumatized children in families (and taking into account the concerns that they may have for the future), we have to begin by acknowledging their previous pain and upset. These children have legitimate and appropriate worries that need to be worked through with people the child has a relationship with, and who they know they can trust. Children placed within SACCS have this relationship with their key carer, who has a central role in their lives. For other children it will be important to identify such a person. Only then can we talk positively to children about what a different family may offer, which will need to be a step-by-step process – perhaps starting with dismissing different family experiences, before considering issues of structure, location and lifestyle.

Questions

- Why are families important?
- How can families benefit traumatized children?
- What are the differences that traumatized children will look for in a family?
- How can fostering be a therapeutic tool?

CHAPTER 2

Children and Their Histories

The effects of trauma

Trauma can be caused by any number of things, some of which reach back even to the child's time in the womb: a very difficult birth or a mother being physically abused when she is pregnant. If a mother smokes, drinks alcohol or takes drugs when pregnant this is also likely to have a deleterious effect on her unborn child, and can result in anything from poor birth weight to brain injury. Poor care in pregnancy and the mother's emotional instability can also have negative effects on the foetus. After birth, in her very first days a baby can be adversely affected (and, in severe cases traumatized) if she is separated from her mother, if her mother shows a lack of interest in her, or if her father is absent or she lacks support. Ziegler (2002) sums up trauma as being 'anything that disrupts the optimal development of a child.'

This range of negative effects together with the fragility of the unborn and newborn child mean that severe physical, mental, emotional or sexual abuse (and, most commonly, a combination of two or more of these) can have devastating effects on a child's growth and development. A child does not have to be beaten about the head for her brain to be affected: neural pathways can also be affected by other forms of physical abuse, as well as by neglect and sexual abuse.[5]

Ziegler (2002) says that 'the most serious finding' of the past decade is that neglect of a child by its caregiver has the most long-lasting effect on development and is the 'most persistent and pervasive' form of trauma. According to him:

> The concern is not only how the brain reacts to neglect as a threat to survival, but also what the brain is *not* doing while preoccupied in

survival mode. Neglect shifts the focus of the infant away from the exploration and essential learning the brain is prepared to do at the beginning of life. (p.37)

However, how different children are affected by trauma will differ according to the severity, cause, the child's age, and the circumstances in which the trauma occurred. But children are also individuals, with their own in-built strengths and resilience, their weak and their strong points. Thus, while *all* trauma has a negative effect, *some* kinds of trauma affect *some* children in *different* ways. James (1994) tells us that:

Psychological trauma occurs when an actual or perceived threat of a danger overwhelms a person's usual coping ability. Many situations that are generally highly stressful to children might not be traumatising to a particular child; some are able to cope and, even if the situation is repeated or chronic, are not developmentally challenged. The diagnosis of traumatisation should be based on the context and meaning of the child's experience, not just on the event alone. What may appear to be a relatively benign experience from an adult perspective – such as a child getting 'lost' for several hours during a family outing – can be traumatising to a youngster. Conversely, a child held hostage with her family at gunpoint might not comprehend the danger and feel relatively safe. (pp.10–11)

It is literally true that trauma is 'overwhelming' because, in the clinical sense, it is far more devastating and means much more than its popular meaning of a severe shock. Its effects may be, at times, uncontrollable. They may, literally, include helplessness, vulnerability to the point of a fear for one's life, experiencing a loss of safety so that one feels wary of others, and a loss of control so that one's actions become unpredictable.

A child's sense of identity, development, her trust in others, her ability to manage her behaviour and so on can also be affected by trauma. Although adults can also be traumatized (sometimes with the same severe and devastating effects as on children) a child's vulnerability can cause her to be affected by trauma in a much more far-reaching way because, since she is still developing physically and emotionally, her general social and individual functioning may well be seriously impaired.

A child's memory may be deeply affected by traumatic experiences – which may be suppressed or distorted or, on the other hand, so crystal clear that the traumatic incident can be remembered in all its horrifying detail. One way that children try to cope with this is through magical thinking, as Fahlberg (2003) explains:

> For the preschool child it is their magical and egocentric thinking that most affects the reaction to parent loss. These children think they caused the loss, and that it came about because of their wishes, thoughts or behaviors. Their propensity for magical thinking is usually reinforced by a loss and is, therefore, likely to persist long beyond the age at which it commonly subsides. (p.138)

Adults hold responsibility for trying to identify the specific magical thinking of the child they are working with or through parenting. What does the child think she did that caused the move? Or what could the child have done to prevent it? What does she think could be done to have the desired outcome? These are questions the adult, not the child, must answer.

Fahlberg (2003) continues that magical thinking sometimes:

> takes place on an unconscious basis, particularly when it reflects the "good vs bad" or the "big vs little" struggles so commonly associated with this developmental stage [preschool years]. Behaviors may provide clues to the child's misperceptions. Carers, both before and after the move, should listen for comments that seem to make no sense, noting any odd or peculiar statements or behaviors. If carefully examined, these frequently give clues as to this child's perceptions and magical thinking. (p.138)

Fahlberg is talking about those children making the 'journey through placement' but what she says is equally applicable to other severe and far-reaching disruptions suffered by children.

Magical thinking is a way children fill in the gaps in their knowledge. When they don't know, they make it up. For example, a foster placement breaks down and the child is moved to a new home but why did the breakdown happen? If the child blames herself for the breakdown (as she may well do), then she will conclude the same again when the next breakdown occurs (as well it might). It is safer for the child to believe this but it only adds to her confusion about why she is where she is. The effect of this is carried through life – children who have filled the gaps in their own lives with their own fantasies, theories and stories do not become adults who are suddenly apprised of the truth. Life-story work helps to give meaning to magical thinking, of why children believe what they have believed to be the truth about their lives, to understand distortion, and it allows them to confront their demons (see p. 54 and Rose and Philpot 2005).

Children who have been abused are also very likely to have a confused view of family relationships (Rose and Philpot 2005), as well as an ever-changing group of people in their lives – which, ironically, is not diminished when they go into care, given the strong possibility of their being placed with a variety of foster carers and residential placements, and experiencing a changing round of social workers. Events like this on top of trauma can lead children to feel that they have no control over their lives. Attempted solutions to this problem can have disastrous consequences, for example, by their becoming suicidal or, at very least, self-harming and self-abusing; by, for instance, taking drugs, or engaging in promiscuous and potentially harmful sexual relationships. The child may develop serious anti-social behaviour to defend her against feelings of vulnerability, but these often only exacerbate her difficulties.

A state of helplessness may also be reverted to. Children may avoid intimacy, feeling that they need to be in control, and acting in ways that deter relationships and closeness with others. They can experience flash-backs, hyperactivity, and dissociation. (This term is what Hunter (2001) calls 'an internal psychological state which we assume is present when a usual or expected involvement of emotion is absent' (p.98).) These, in turn, can affect their education and lead them to be diagnosed with various behavioural disorders.

James (1994) lists the four major effects of trauma on children as:

- a persistent state of fear
- disordered memory
- avoiding intimacy, and
- 'dysregulation of affect'.[6]

Trauma can also have a very serious effect on attachment, which can adversely affect a child's emotional development and her ability to make relationships with others. Attachment has been described by Howe (2000) as 'an instinctive biological drive that propels infants into protective proximity with their main carers whenever they experience anxiety, fear or distress' (p.26). Bowlby (1969) argues that we will develop maturely when our attachment stems from a nurturing and loving relationship, but that when the relationship is one based on violence, rejection, pain, abuse, lack of bonding and disruption (that is, one that gives rise to the possibility of traumatic experiences) then there will be problems in future relationships – in extreme cases, entailing criminal, violent or abusive sexual behaviour.[7]

Ziegler (2002) describes one kind of reaction to trauma when he says:

> For traumatized individuals, emotions have lost their usefulness in providing important information to the reasoning centres of the neocortex, and emotions become a runaway train that catapults the child into the past and face-to-face with previous traumatic experiences. It is not effective to say to a traumatized child: 'Calm down, you are overreacting.' You might as well say this to a passenger on a plane that is coming in for an emergency landing. Who are you to decide what is overreacting? (p.150)

With 'flight' the child cries and alerts caregivers to seek protection. Tantrums and aggressive behaviour can be the strategy of flight for terrorized children. But since children are mostly unable to flee situations they fear, they commonly resort to dissociation.

'Freezing' is usually seen as the child being oppositional or defiant. When negative, defiant, disobedient or hostile behaviour is shown toward authority figures it is considered to be signs of a conduct disorder. This includes signs and symptoms such as temper tantrums, arguing with adults, actively defying rules, deliberately annoying people, unfairly blaming others for mistakes or misbehaviour, or being touchy, easily annoyed, angry, resentful, spiteful or vindictive. The adult response to all of these can be to threaten and make demands, which simply increase the child's fear.

Van der Kolk, McFarlane and Weisaeth (1996) have developed theories about the somatic aspects of trauma. Traditional psychotherapy, according to van der Kolk (2002), pays scant regard to post-traumatic bodily experiences. New understandings about the brain show that emotional states originate in our physical condition: for example, our body's chemical profile, the state of the internal organs, the contraction of the muscles in our face, throat, trunk and limbs. The most common and obvious manifestation of this is how we shake and perspire and our breathing rate increases dramatically in stressful situations. van der Kolk (2002) claims that these findings should promote our awareness, rather than our avoidance of somatic states:

> Mindfulness, awareness of one's inner experience is necessary for a person to respond according to what is happening and is needed in the present, rather than reacting to certain somatic sensations as a return of the traumatic past. Such awareness will free people to introduce new options to solve problems and not merely to react reflexively. (p.50)

For van der Kolk, part of working with those who are traumatized involves helping them regain bodily control by reworking the trauma and completing the action. In an interview with Pointon (2004), he says:

> It's via the awareness of deep bodily experience that people can begin to move around the way that they feel – not by keeping it out there. The story of what happened is worth telling, but to change your reaction to it, you have to go via the deep internal felt sense.

The trauma bond

The trauma bond (also sometimes called the Stockholm Syndrome[8]) refers to a bond that can develop, in extreme cases, between abductees and their kidnappers. This trauma bond is most associated in the popular imagination with Patty Hearst, heir to the US publishing company founded by her grandfather, William Randolph Hearst. A group calling itself the Symbionese Liberation Army kidnapped her and she ended up as one of 'them', taking part, apparently uncoerced, in bank robberies. This identification with her captors became so extreme that it was symbolized in her being renamed Tania.

This phenomenon illustrates how trauma can operate deceptively at times and have the semblance of a secure attachment within a family. But the trauma bond and secure attachment differ in that attachment is based on love and the trauma bond is based on fear and distorts the child's perceptions. The child lives in a state of underlying uncertainty, dependency and apprehension and so seeks to appease the abuser – to meet, even anticipate his needs and demands. Children affected by the trauma bond exhibit behaviour that is geared to meeting the needs of the adult or what they perceive those needs are. This state is similar to the concept of 'false self' defined by Winnicott (1966) as a state in which the child's aim is to protect herself by complying with the wishes of another and hence denying the needs of her real self. When a child grows to adulthood, how she conducts relationships will be shaped by these experiences, which suggests that these relationships will be conducted in a state of servility and dependence. A victim mentality can also result from this and the child, now growing to maturity, can become attracted to (and invite relationships with) powerful people who cause harm and help to reinforce her view of relationships. The trauma bond can also determine how adults view themselves as parents.

Ziegler (2002) writes of the trauma bond:

> It may seem strange to say that survival can be promoted in negative ways, but this idea is the reality for many abused children. These children develop negative bonds that promote their survival, which are called loyalty bonds or trauma bonds. If someone holds your life in their hands, they are very relevant and powerful to you. Pleasing such a person, or at least not displeasing them, becomes critical. Such an experience can rapidly change an individual in lasting ways. The rape victim, the prisoner of war, the hostage, and the abused child all have similar experiences.

> Severely abused children have nothing else to compare with, so what is happening to them seems not to be unusual; indeed it is usual. Thus, even when the situation comes to an end, they may not be able to feel that the trauma is over and so their loyalty to their abuser may continue and the bond remains as a response to a life-threatening situation. This is a challenge to a foster carer in the responses he can offer. Love is not enough and what will be required are different parenting styles and techniques (p.84).

'Over-active stress responses' in traumatized children have been observed by Perry and Szalavitz (2006). This can make the children needy, aggressive and impulsive. This means that time and patience are essential when working with them. The writers go on:

> These children are difficult, they are easy to upset and hard to calm, they may overact to the slightest novelty or change and they don't know how to think before they act. Before they can make any kind of lasting change at all in their behavior, they need to feel safe and loved. Unfortunately, however, many of the treatment programs and other interventions aimed at them get it backwards: they take a punitive approach and hope to lure children into good behavior by restoring love and safety only if the children first start acting 'better'. While such approaches may temporarily threaten children into doing what adults want, they can't provide the long-term, internal motivation that will ultimately help them control themselves better and become more loving toward others. (p.244)

Fostering and trauma

Trauma does not just go away, even with the best therapy in the world. Children coming to family placement carry their trauma with them. The manner in which it is acted out will depend on a number of things including:

- the severity of the trauma
- the recovery treatment and therapeutic process undertaken
- the parenting skills and understanding of the carer
- the understanding of the child; and
- the understanding of the carer about himself.

A variety of approaches and techniques has been developed by different people to allow traumatized children to be fostered successfully (for example, see Archer and Burnell 2003; Maginn 2006). This includes multi-dimensional foster care, as now practised in the United Kingdom.[9] Emphases in these approaches may differ but the essential component is the recognition of the need for safety, security and containment as preconditions for the re-learning of attachment.

However, the general and loose use of phrases like 'attachment disorder' and 'lacking attachment' can lead to a simplistic approach to helping children. An editorial in *Adopted Child* (1994) stated that a variety of attachment disorders require a variety of treatments and quoted Magid as saying that a child's ability to build a reciprocal relationship with a parent or caregiver is dependent not only on the experiences that the child has with the caregiver but also on 'the child's biologic [*sic*] and neurologic [*sic*] makeup'.

For recovery to be successful, we may need to work in a number of ways – which may include a therapeutic approach that uses one or more techniques (including, for example, music, art or expressive therapies) alongside, for example, cognitive behavioural therapy. It is the combination of these approaches, sometimes described as 'multi-system therapy' that is effective (Tomlinson and Philpot 2008).

Questions

- How do you think a mother's experiences can negatively affect her unborn child?

- Name three effects of trauma.

- How can trauma appear to be a form of attachment and why is this?

Multiple moves

Unfortunately, the experiences of children and young people in care who have suffered abuse and trauma do not encourage children to believe that families can offer them security, care and safety. We have already said that the birth family will have been the place where these children have undergone the experiences that have brought them into care. But to then place them in foster care may only confirm, for different reasons, their negative view of family life. This is because their progress through the care system is often not with just one family but, all too frequently, with many different ones. It is not uncommon for such children to have had 10, 20, 30 or even more placements by the time they start school. Inappropriately placing severely traumatized children in foster care aggravates their problems and leads to fostering breakdown, a change of placement, further breakdown and then into a spiral where the child's problems not only worsen and are aggravated by change but family placement appears to her to be the least attractive of options. Such a history breeds in the child concerned a strong sense of rejection, unending (and often unanswered) questions about whether she is to blame for these failures, and a rejection and distrust of any who attempt to care for her in future.

Children are often offered confusing and sometimes damaging explanations and rationalizations for multiple moves, including: that it was only a short-term placement; that she was going on holiday; that it is better that she does not remain in the placement; and that she doesn't get on with the foster carers' own child or children.

Often these comments are made by carers or others in order to mitigate the real situation and their feelings of guilt evoked from failing a child. The carer may, in reality, feel that the child is just like her birth parents and will end up in prison, or is violent and aggressive.

The child in these circumstances develops an arousal cycle that is dysfunctional. To adapt a concept from Fahlberg (2003), she experiences a heightened need, which, in turn, produces high anxiety/arousal that is not resolved. The continuing anxiety and arousal then lead to feelings of panic, which, in turn, lead to deterioration in behaviour. The impact of this is to make the child become untrusting and rejecting, and to feel isolated. The world, she feels, is not a safe, secure, contained place. It cannot be trusted and neither can people, because each move builds on negative experience of the last one and makes a child more and more unlikely to attach. Yet many children continue to be placed routinely in foster home after foster home in the hope that they'll stick somewhere. In reality, this produces children whose attachment relationships have been so disrupted that they develop abnormal patterns of attachment. They believe that families are unsafe and insecure, at one extreme offering abuse and damage and at the other being unable to manage the child or her behaviour and thus making her feel more unsafe and insecure.

It is far too simplistic, when dealing with severely emotionally damaged children and young people, to say that 'families are best' as this is in direct contradiction of their internal working model, which tells them that families are dangerous, harmful and unresponsive. Being moved from foster family to foster family tells them that families are untrustworthy; that there is no point in becoming attached because they will be moved; and it is better to make the move sooner, rather than later. This is not a skewed view of the world; it is a perfectly rational conclusion for a child to draw in such circumstances.

The aim of the work with the child, therefore, should be to help the child be prepared to take the risk to balance the opportunities offered by a family placement against the risks associated with previous experiences in their birth family and past inappropriate placements. This can be a difficult process. The consequence of multiple rejections in relationships is that there is greater safety in a more impersonal environment of bricks and mortar, such as a residential care home.

The injuries suffered by children are so profound – to their person, their innocence, their emotional and spiritual well-being, and their belief in their right to grow up in their own families – that they affect both children's external and internal worlds. They require the integrated approach of therapeutic parenting, individual therapy and life-story work, which addresses the harm at the most basic level and focuses on children's recovery.

When foster care is inappropriate – as it is for a profoundly damaged child – then residential care offers a chance to work with the child in a secure and safe environment. Integral to a child's recovery and her ability to benefit eventually from foster care is the acknowledgment of her negative view of families and the reasons for this, and to work with her on that through an integrated approach. In this way the child is helped to step out of the negative cycle of sabotaging placements and preventing herself from receiving help, and from believing that a family is to be avoided.

Questions

- What are the negative affects on a child of multiple moves in care?

- What could be the effect of placing a severely traumatized child straight into a foster home?

- What are the advantages for traumatized children of a first placement in residential care?

- How can children, damaged by their own families, be helped to believe that an eventual placement with a family will benefit them?

An integrated approach

After residential care, the child takes her next step in the recovery process – placement with a family. However, this process is not a linear one. It is one characterized by recovery progress and a set of achievements, and then some regression, as the child integrates, and, on occasions, battles against the newly emerging inner working model (which we go on to describe in Chapter 4). This is the mechanism through which the child attempts to connect her self, other people and the relationship between them. It is how she understands the world and her place in it. The quality of the child's caring experiences will determine whether this internal working model is positive or negative.

In working with a child the integrated approach has three parts: life-story work; therapy; and therapeutic parenting.
They do not follow one after the other but are operated simultaneously by the recovery team – which is all those working directly with the child, and includes the therapeutic parenting team (who work with the child in the home) the child's therapist and life-story worker.

Key to the SACCS' integrated model are:

- safety (in place of fear)

- containment (in place of disintegration), and

- attachment (in place of detachment).

Thus, the model is based on:

- openness, not secrecy

- communication, not avoidance; and

- predictability, not inconsistency.

It is important to stress that all of this applies to fostering and placement as much as to any other service that helps the child, and that family placement staff are part of the recovery team.

As the approach is integrated, and members work as a team, communication must be open and clearly defined, flowing between the therapeutic parenting team, the therapists and the life-story workers. In addition, all members of the recovery team should on a regular basis appraise, update and share with the referring local authority all new insights, strategies or anxieties with the referring local authority that occur between reviews or designated contact visits on a regular basis.

Therapy

Therapy is perhaps the best known, but most commonly misunderstood, aspect of the three elements that make up the integrated model (Rymaszewska and Philpot 2006).

The therapist, working in the space between the inner and outer world of the child as unconscious images emerge in symbolic form, builds a relationship with the child in which the therapist can begin to explore that inner world. By making use, for example, of techniques like play, music, art, dance and drama the therapist can help the child slowly examine some of the harmful experiences of her past. It is the task of the therapist to assist the child in unravelling her confused and overwhelming feelings, containing her as she does so, and helping her to externalize those feelings so that they cease to have power over her.

The therapist helps the child to reprocess her experiences by addressing the distortions in her thinking, so that the past can fall into perspective. Life-story work (see below) informs that understanding of past experiences and people, and therapeutic parenting (see below) forms the secure base upon which the therapeutic healing can take place.

Therapy is often associated with the idea of client–therapist confidentiality and this is entirely appropriate in the most common forms of therapy whereby the patient or client attends the therapist's consulting room for a certain amount of time each week or each month. However, given the context of this book, it should be pointed out that in a residential setting, therapy is one of the elements of the overall therapeutic provision, and this means that, unlike in a clinical outpatient setting, therapists cannot practise with the same degree of privacy or confidentiality – or rather that confidentiality takes a different form. This is because all members of the recovery team – those involved in life-story work and therapeutic parenting – need to know what is happening in the therapy session and how a child is behaving and reacting. Likewise, therapeutic parents and life-story workers share information with their therapist colleagues. Thus, the whole team shares confidentiality.

Therapeutic provision in family placement will follow the same rules and guidelines as those offered in residential care. In order for the recovery process to continue for the child in family placement then foster carers, life-story workers and therapists will share information with their colleagues in the recovery team. Confidentiality is shared by the teams and operates here in the same way as in other parts of the fostering process. For example, carers cannot promise children and young people that they will not share information or disclosures.

Therapy in family placement is complex, and is one part of the jigsaw. The nature of the therapy offered – individual, family, therapeutic consultation, cognitive or psychodynamic and other therapies – will be based around individual needs. However, the prescription is that there will be an oversight of the therapeutic process, and that the provision of this is, therefore, not indicative of a problem, more a recognition of continuing issues. (This is a theme we will return to when looking at placement support.)

In this book we make various references to all three parts of the recovery team – the life-story worker, the therapist and the therapeutic parent – but it should be emphasized again that they are working hand in hand, each sharing knowledge about the child, even when the child is, at certain times, in the care of different members of the team. This means that a child who is undergoing therapy will, at the same time, be experiencing therapeutic parenting and undertaking the journey that is life-story work.

Life-story work

Although life-story work with children who are to be adopted is well established in social work (Ryan and Walker 2003) (and some work of this kind is carried out with older people (Gibson 2004; Haight 1998)), the life-story work referred to here is richer, deeper and more detailed, and takes considerably more time. It involves the child in both gathering some of the evidence, telling her story, selecting materials to illustrate that story, and writing or helping to write the story itself (Rose and Philpot 2005).

Life-story work seeks to answer not only the questions of what, why, and when about the child's life, but also who – who helped the child and who harmed her? Only when children have the answers to all these questions can they express how they feel about what has happened to them. Although Connor, Sclare, Dunbar and Elliffe (1985) were talking about life-story work and adoption, their description of what the life story is about fits well with what we are describing here. It is, they say, about 'unravelling confusion and discarding some of the negative emotional baggage which the child has carried for so long'.

Life-story work attaches importance to the past. However, the past is seen as *part* of the therapeutic process – as something much more than merely chronological or even factual. As Rose and Philpot (2005) say: 'Life-story work is about the people in the child's life, what happened to the child and the reasons why those things happened. It is not, and cannot be a simple narrative or description' (p. 16). Life-story work takes away from the child responsibility for what happened to her and places it where it belongs – with the adult who abused her. However, during her family placement the child may question her responsibility and how safe she feels, which may require a continuation of life-story work.

Life-story work involves interviewing people who have been part of the child's life, from family to foster carers, social workers to parents, residential workers to teachers. It involves reading social work and court reports; searching out official documents like birth, marriage and death certificates, and electoral registers; visiting (sometimes with the child) places where she has lived or which are significant to her; talking with the child at great length and liaising with her current carers (therapist, foster parents and residential workers); drawing up both family trees and ecocharts (see pp.106–107 Rose and Philpot 2005); as well as helping the child create their life-story book.

Life-story work is based on the belief that none of us can ignore what has happened in the past and then just move on. This is even more the case with traumatized children, for to ignore their past and try to move on would be impossible because the past would then always overshadow their present. The past must be faced, analysed, understood and, finally, accepted. Only then is progress – recovery – possible.

However, it is important to note that life-story work is not something that has an end – not just a means of preparing the child for placement. It is something that continues into placement and is carried out by the foster carer, regularly supported by the life-story worker. Up to the time of placement, life story is a way of helping a child to understand what has happened to her and to help her to learn that she is not responsible for that. This enables her to look toward to the future, and fostering placement is part of that future, a step back into the world of everyday. The role of the foster carer in life story is to help the child relate what happens now to what has happened in the past. A memory may be triggered by something as commonplace as a television programme and it then becomes the task of the foster carer to help the child, if she wants to, to reflect on this and its meaning to her.

So far as family placement is concerned, life-story work continues in family placement because placement continues as part of the recovery process. The work done there may not be as intensive as much of the exploratory and investigative work that has been done so far but under-standing changes over time, and fresh memories recur. There are also other ways in which this happens. While in foster care, children are once again living in a family with all its worries and anxieties, and memories from the past. Our experience is that often children are reminded of their past times in families by small events. While living in a family, a child's life-story book is therefore continued and developed, enabling children and young people to continue their life-story development.

Therapeutic parenting

The third and equally important part of the integrated model is therapeutic parenting (Pughe and Philpot 2007). Children whose abuse and neglect has been severe will have attachment problems because of interference with their emotional development and their associated negative experiences. Part of the therapeutic response to this is to compensate for deficiencies in their parenting with a therapeutic regime that is accepting and containing. They are being 're-parented' because the structured help that they require gives as near as possible an approximation to the kind of positive parenting that they should have received. Therapeutic parenting is not only about the creation of a physical environment reminiscent of an ordinary home; it is also the kind of care, in large and small everyday things, that the 'good enough' parent would have given to the child. It is the team of carers who work in the residential home who carry out the task of therapeutic parenting but, again, therapeutic parenting continues into the foster placement.

The majority of children who have been abused will not have received the emotional and physical nurture that is necessary for their healthy development. This early privation or deprivation has left them with critical gaps in their emotional development; they may be left emotionally frozen or fragmented, and have an internal working model that severely impairs their ability to form healthy attachments. Therapeutic parenting aims to provide a child with an experience of parenting that offers symbolic and actual experiences which seek to fill the gaps in her development. In time, this provision will challenge the child's inner working model and enable her to begin to feel differently about herself, other people and the world around her.

An essential part of this work is the opportunity for a child to develop a primary attachment with one person, her key carer. It is through this primary attachment that a child will be able to experience a level of preoccupation (akin to the maternal preoccupation normally associated with infancy) through which her recovery can take place (Winnicott 1992). A key carer, supported by the recovery team, will ensure that all a child's physical, emotional and therapeutic needs are met.

The environment where the child now lives is in itself a therapeutic opportunity and one that is psychologically, as well as physically, significant. Every part of a child's life is seen as having therapeutic potential and, therefore, in order to reflect this the residential and fostering home is structured with great attention to everyday details. For children who may have been deprived of so much, emotionally and physically, the home should have a sense of plenty being available: toys, games, art, ornaments, plants, furnishings, comics and books. It should be child-centred and reflect the personalities and needs of the children who live there. In residential care the children live in small, family-based homes for up to five children and a care team of ten, giving the children the opportunity to develop relationships within a protected environment. Through internalizing their attachments and the experiences that children undergo in an accepting environment with therapeutic parenting, they are able to reach a level of recovery which enables them to move successfully on to family placement and to achieving their potential.

The model of therapeutic parenting that is practised in residential care is transferred to family placement. The carers need, therefore, to practise not conventional parenting, but *therapeutic* parenting – which is a key skill in successfully fostering traumatized and attachment-distorted children. This kind of parenting requires specialist skills and training.

Having been parented successfully in residential care in this way, the sense of safety, security and containment that comes from this is a factor in the successful transition to family placement. The move is not just a move to family placement but rather a continuation of the successful parenting style, but in a different location. The re-parenting discussed in Pughe and Philpot (2007), therefore, continues in the kind of setting in which previous poor parenting occurred, thus challenging the child's previous internal working model and confirming the newly emerging internal working model.

Identifying young people who are ready to move on

As we have mentioned, local authority practices promote the goal that no child under 12 should be placed in residential care. This means that the most appropriate kind of placement for a child is not assessed because these policies assume that families offer the best placement opportunity for all children, particularly young ones.

The severe abuse and trauma that some children have undergone within families contributes to foster care breakdown, as we have stated earlier (Berridge and Cleaver 1987; Farmer *et al.* 2004; Kelly and Gilligan 2000; Sinclair 2005). In 2002, a SACCS survey revealed that the majority of the children placed in residential care with the agency had, on average, experienced 9 placements – which had exacerbated their original trauma. Such children are not suitable to be placed in a family because of their destructive abilities and their own entrenched internal working model of families.

Through the process of recovery a child begins to make progress, which is monitored through continuing assessment (Tomlinson and Philpot

2008). However, there will come a time when a child has made sufficient progress within residential care (aided by therapy, life-story work and therapeutic parenting) that she can move to a family placement. But when exactly is this point reached and how do we know it has been?

A child's developmental process can be understood through rigorous assessment. Assessment offers the indicators of learning, physical development, emotional development, attachment, identity and social communication. Each of these indicators is scored in comparison to those of a healthy child of a similar age (Tomlinson and Philpot 2008). The assessment helps to:

- identify where a child has reached in terms of development

- measure her progress and outcomes

- provide consistent evidence progress and outcomes

- work out plans within the context of achieving outcomes

- communicate about outcomes clearly; and

- evaluate our approaches as to what works and what does not.

Integrated working (see above), within a residential setting, allows the child to feel safe, contained and protected. She is then encouraged to challenge her own internal working model. At times this can cause her to behave destructively and so demand very high levels of support. If the child is not supported at this time she can revert to her previous behaviour very quickly and most of the work done so far is destroyed, requiring it to be carried out again.

This challenging of the child's understanding and defence mechanisms can leave her very vulnerable as the old understanding breaks down while the new understanding has yet to be internalized. This period of transition – the challenging of the internal working model and the replacement of old understanding by new understanding – is one of uncertainty for the child. It can make her susceptible to retreating to previous behaviours because they are familiar, at a time when she's feeling exposed and defenceless.

It is often at times of change, when there is strong containment and behaviour is seen as managed, that local authorities feel that the child has changed sufficiently to make her ready for a family placement. However, we believe that the change at this stage is not sufficient for this to take place successfully: such change as there has been is only a start and the process of internalization needs to continue.

We can use a model borrowed from the business world (Mumford 1994) to describe what happens here:

- Children move from feeling afraid of families and having a negative internal working model (*unconsciously incompetent*) to

- being made aware that such a view is mistaken although they will still not have tested that view (*consciously incompetent*).

- They then move to being able to recognize that the world is different but are always thinking about the world and the reactions of others (*consciously competent*)

- which then leads a changed view of the world, themselves and their responsibilities and a positive internal working model (*unconsciously competent*). This is the beginning of their internalization.

With these new experiences in the contained environment of residential care the child now reaches a stage where she has begun to recognize that outcomes can be different. She can begin to change attitudes and behaviour due to the continuing positive experiences that are provided from the contained environment.

She has, however, not *fully* internalized these new experiences and the stress of finding herself living in a family again can create in her the trauma response of freeze, fight and flight, which can lead to regression in her behaviour. One example here would be a child who, praised by her carer for looking pretty, cuts her hair because she doesn't like being praised for how she looks.

There is, therefore, a need at this time to concentrate on the process of internalization of reactions, as the child begins to understand her new internal working model. These then become the routine positive reactions with which she is familiar. This process can take a very long time and can be characterized by periods of growth and regression. Gradually she begins to feel safe and contained as a result of the safety and containment given her by the environment.

From what we know of this process as it occurs in children, attempts to identify whether the child is ready to move on need to begin 15 to 18 months in advance of the need for a placement. This is so that the key carer, life-story worker, therapist and social worker can produce as accurate a profile of the child as possible, as well as a realistic description of the types of family she could live in. The mechanism for providing this information is the SACCS Recovery Programme (whereby children are measured and assessed regularly), and the provision of professional review and placement planning meetings at 23 months, and regularly thereafter to review progress (Tomlinson and Philpot 2008).

However, an assessment of the process of internalization by children ready for family placement may show that while they are not ready for such a placement full time they could benefit from what is called 'practice family placement' (see Chapter 5), as a way of further embedding their new internal model.

Questions

- You are to meet a friend in a foreign country that you have never visited before and where you will be staying for a few days. But when you arrive, there is a message from your friend to say that he cannot come because of an accident. You know nothing of the geography of the country, let alone the town. You do not speak the language and are unfamiliar with local customs. You know no one there. Think about comparisons of this situation with that of a child who is placed with a family.

- What do you think are three qualities that should be sought in a foster carer? What three qualities might make you doubt that an applicant would be a suitable carer?

- Think of three things in a family that might lead a child to believe that she was unsafe and not adequately protected?

CHAPTER 3

The Carers

Foster carers: who are they?

If foster care is the backbone of children's services, then foster carers are the marrow in that bone. And yet we know much less about them than we do about other people who work with children and young people. They have been subject to fewer surveys and research than these other groups. However, Triseliotis, Borland and Hill (2000), drawing on various published and official sources, do much to clarify matters. Estimates they reported at the time of their publication put the number of fostering households at 23,454 in England and of these at least 2,707 (12 per cent) were relatives, and 454 worked in independent agencies. In Scotland there were 1,923 fostering households, 226 of whom were relatives and 54 working with independent agencies.

Figures for fostering households are not available after 2000 but we do know that in England at 31 March 2007 of the 60,000 children and young people in care, 42,000 (72 per cent) were fostered (Department for Children, Schools and Families 2008). In Scotland there were 14,060 children and young people in care, of whom 4,055 (29 per cent) were in foster care (Scottish Assembly 2007), while Wales had 3,465 (74.7 per cent) of its 4,640 care population with foster carers (BAAF Adoption and Fostering 2008). In Northern Ireland there were 2,356 looked-after children and young people in care at 31 March 2007 and 1,522 (62.5 per cent) were in foster care at the same time a year earlier (Department of Health, Social Services and Public Safety 2008).

But who is a foster carer? How do they compare with the average citizen? What are their family patterns? There have been five comprehensive studies of foster carers, the first as long ago as 1957 (Gray and Parr 1957). Ames (1993) provided the second study. The third study, by Warren (1997), painted a portrait which showed that:

- 90 per cent of foster carers had homes with three or more bedrooms
- 66 per cent of fostering households had one partner working full time and the other partner not employed
- 80 per cent of female carers were aged 31–55 years of age
- 12.5 per cent of foster families had their own birth child aged under five
- 90 per cent were two-parent families
- Nearly 25 per cent were working in caring or child-related professions such as teaching, social work and nursing
- 5 per cent of carers were black.

Warren also went on to report that a general desire to help children needing care was a strong motivation for becoming a foster carer. He found 'many' carers had been unable to have children, had been advised not to have more or were intentionally childless. But he also found that female foster carers tended to have more children than other women of comparable age and marital status.

Some of these findings are not surprising but the numbers of black carers is less than half of the percentage of black children in care. The number of carers who work in, or came from, the caring and child-related professions was highlighted by Sellick and Connolly (2001). They found that independent fostering agencies are finding a new class of foster carer, who swaps over from working as a salaried caring professional to become a foster carer for an independent fostering agency.

The fourth study of foster carers is that by Triseliotis *et al.* (2000) who looked at 800 carers. While this study does give a profile of today's foster carer, it is based on research in Scotland. However, allowing for the point made below about the possible number of carers who are from ethnic minorities, there is little reason to believe that this is not a representative profile of all carers. (Other exceptions are that Scottish carers are more likely also to be single, in non-manual jobs and connected with a job in social care.)

Triseliotis and his colleagues (2000) tell us the following:

- Most carers start fostering when aged between 31 and 40. But these figures also show differences between authority areas – in one place 27 per cent of carers were in the age range of 41–50 but in another only 4 per cent fell into that age group.

- Seventy-nine per cent were married, 4 per cent were single and had never been married, 6 per cent were widowed, and 11 per cent were divorced or separated. (The authors compare this with Bebbington and Miles' findings in 1990 that 87 per cent of foster households in England had two parents.) Again, there were variations from one place to another – 31 per cent of carers in one authority were on their own but in another area the number was only 10 per cent. The authors speculate that in England it is likely that there will be higher proportions of single carers among those from ethnic minority carers.

- Fewer lone carers than couples had their own children living at home, but while they had less space in their homes, they were more likely to foster slightly more children at any one time than were couples.

- Only 8 per cent of foster carers had no children of their own and the others had an average of three, though not all lived at home. (The researchers mention the finding of Gray and Parr (1957) who found that 37 per cent of carers were childless.)

- A tenth of carers had one or more adopted children and the same number had one or more stepchildren, though the authors think both figures an underestimate.

- Ninety-nine per cent of carers described themselves as white. The 1991 Census in Scotland found that 1 per cent of the population listed themselves as black, Pakistani, Indian or Chinese, and in some cities the percentage would be likely to be higher. However, given that in England the percentage of people from an ethnic minority is much higher than in Scotland and the proportion of black foster carers, though not high enough in numbers, is disproportionate to their numbers in the general population, this is a finding that cannot be applied to England.

- Sixty-two per cent of those surveyed indicated 'the mainstream Protestant Church' (that is, the Church of Scotland) as their affiliation, 17 per cent were Catholics and nearly one in ten were attached to other mainstream Christian churches.

- Sixty-eight per cent of the carers were homeowners and 20 per cent lived in local authority housing. The typical foster carer owned a three-bed semi-detached house with an enclosed garden.

- Ninety per cent said they were in good health and 60 per cent said that their health was 'very good'.

- In 16 per cent of cases both carers smoked and in 44 per cent only one did. Forty per cent of carers did not smoke.

- Over 80 per cent of carers were car owners – which compared with the 59 per cent of Scottish householders who had a car in 1993.

- Seventeen per cent of the men and 20 per cent of the women had stayed on at school past the official leaving age and the numbers holding an O-level pass or Highers was lower than in the general population in 1992. Twenty-nine per cent of both men and women carers had obtained a qualification after leaving school, the majority of which were vocational.

- Seventy-two per cent of men and 37 per cent of women were employed and of the female carers who worked outside the home, 60 per cent worked part time. In two-carer homes, 38 per cent of the men and 34 per cent of the women worked; in 15 per cent of such homes no one worked and in 7 per cent only the woman worked. Six per cent consisted of two retired carers.

The fifth study (Sinclair, Gibbs and Wilson, 2004) points out that while the social characteristics of carers varied by local authority, overall however,

there was little difference between characteristics in this sample and those studied by Gray and Parr in the 1950s, Bebbington and Miles in the late 1980s, or Triseliotis and his colleagues in the late 1990s. The one major difference related to the proportion of minority ethnic carers – a finding that may reflect the fact that we deliberately chose authorities who were likely to have high ethnic minority populations (which Scotland as a whole does not) or a change in practice since the 1980s. (p.29)

The Social Care Institute for Excellence (2004), summarizing research, says that a majority of carers are married couples who have school-age children but there are considerable variations between and within agencies. There are fewer single carers, working mothers and families with children under five years of age (Bebbington and Miles 1990; Gray and Parr 1957; Sinclair *et al.* 2004; Triseliotis *et al.* 2000).

Sellick (2002), looking at independent fostering agencies, found that of the 1,819 carers surveyed, 1,419 were couples and most of them (1,268) were married. There were comparatively few single carers (403), unmarried couples (134) and very few were same-sex couples. In this survey, the majority of carers were white. However, differences between agencies in these regards can be seen when considering Sinclair *et al.* (2004) who found that the proportion of carers from an ethnic minority background varied between 0 and 75 per cent, while Waterhouse and Brocklesby (1999) found that half of the carers they studied were single.

There is a common view that fostering is a working-class occupation, while adoption is something generally undertaken by middle-class people. Triseliotis *et al.* (2000) mention several studies that disagree about the class background of foster carers – these have found them to be working class, middle class and representative of the general population. Using the Registrar General's Occupational Classification list, and using jobs as an indicator of social class, Triseliotis *et al.* found:

- 1 per cent of women and 6 per cent of men were professional
- 27 per cent of both men and women were managers
- 11 per cent of women and 39 per cent of men were manual
- 28 per cent of women and 16 per cent of men were semi-skilled
- 6 per cent of women and 4 per cent of men were unskilled

- Around two-thirds of female carers were connected with social care – nursing, childminding, social work, teaching, care assistant, home helps, support staff.

Knowing who foster carers are is one thing, but how to recruit them and keep them is another.

Foster carers: finding them, keeping them and matters of reward

Foster carers may not be salaried workers but they share one unfortunate characteristic with others who work in the public services – they are becoming more and more difficult to recruit. Fostering Network estimates that more than 10,000 extra are needed in the UK (Fostering Network 2007). After a Scottish survey in 2005, the total UK shortage was exactly 11,000. This was an increase of 35 per cent from 2002. And when, in 2002, the former Social Services Inspectorate looked at seven local authorities, it found only one that had a sufficient choice of placements to match the needs of all its children requiring foster care. Another was able to place 80 per cent of all children with local foster carers, while all the others had difficulty in making appropriate matches (Department of Health 2002a), this despite the fact that in 2000 the Department had launched a £2 million campaign to recruit an extra 7,000 foster carers.

Social workers, nurses, teachers, police officers and other public-service workers have all been the subject of professional concern; some have provoked prime-ministerial statements, and some have even been the subject of national, government-funded advertising campaigns. The crisis in recruiting foster carers is just as acute and – to take the professional group with whom they are most closely associated – in its own way as serious in its implications for good child care as that of social workers. Indeed, the two can't be separated – the shortage of social workers has serious implications for foster care because the lack of experience in social work and fostering means that expertise can be lost. But analogies between recruiting social workers and other public-service workers and foster carers can only go so far – foster-care recruitment and retention demands different strategies to those used for recruiting these other professionals because the causes of the problem are different, as well as the nature of the group itself being different.

What foster carers are paid affects their recruitment, even if they are not primarily motivated by financial reward. Indeed, one of the unrecognized aspects of the service for young people leaving care is how many foster carers continue to look after them though they are no longer officially in their care and being paid for such.

Being able to recruit sufficient foster carers and retain them is more than the mere equation: 'We have so many children and young people needing foster care, therefore, we need so many foster carers'. Having the right supply of carers of the right *quality* is about ensuring flexibility, of being able to match the children and young people to carers, and of ensuring that those cared for can have appropriate continuing relationships with their families and those whom they know. Government guidance says that carers should foster no more than three children at any one time.

That the inadequate supply of foster carers militates too often against choice is shown by several research studies (see, for example, Berridge and Cleaver 1987; Sinclair, Garnett and Berridge 1995; Triseliotis *et al.* 1995b). What happens, in practice, is that social workers have to make use of the first available placement and not the one that offers the particular skills and expertise needed. A report from the Social Services Inspectorate found that 75 per cent of children had no choice of placement (quoted, Triseliotis *et al.* 2000).

When it comes to children from ethnic-minority backgrounds, the situation is worse. Finding black, and especially Asian carers, is all the more acute a problem. Triseliotis *et al.* (2000) found that in Scotland, two-thirds of African-Caribbean children were fostered in all-white families. But there are sometimes (rare) exceptions to this rule. Shaw and Hipgrave (1989) discovered that some authorities had more black and Asian foster carers than they had black and Asian children to place. Admittedly this was in 1988 but they ask whether 'it is ever appropriate to use black carers for white children, not least as some agencies are finding it easier to recruit black than white carers'.

But why should there be problems with recruitment and retention? Research suggests that there is no one cause. If it were a matter of remuneration, then given the rates that some local authorities pay, women (for it is usually women) who were thinking about fostering could equally be attracted by jobs in, say, residential care. While those jobs are notoriously underpaid, they do have the advantage of paid holidays, sick pay and pensions, while fostering is a full-time job that doesn't bring with it these benefits. While foster care is very satisfying work, it would not appeal to people whose satisfaction also comes from working outside the home. And when both partners in a family work, the remuneration of foster care is rarely enough to tempt the woman to switch jobs.

Other social factors have also influenced recruitment and retention, including the growth of single-parent households, increased family stress, and higher levels of mortgage repossessions (in the 1980s and 1990s). Although we take these as read as part of modern life we don't seem to feed them into the research about why foster carers are so increasingly difficult to come by. Then, too, there, are practical reasons that militate against a choice of foster care as a job – for example, the lack of suitable accommodation and the status of the service.

Ways of recruiting foster carers are well practised – leaflets and posters in places used by the public, like town halls, libraries, and community and health centres. Some London boroughs take advertising on the underground, as well as undertaking door-to-door leafleting. Advertisements are placed in local newspapers and the ethnic-minority press, as well as in council newspapers, which also carry features about fostering. Local television and radio are also a means of reaching the audience. General approaches can work but where particular children have special needs then advertisements sometimes focus on them in the hope of attracting carers to whom they appeal. Advertisements, leaflets and posters also appear in the different languages spoken in an area. All this advertising is often – but should be always – backed up with a dedicated helpline.

However, there is a certain hit and miss attitude to advertising. In their Scottish study, Triseliotis *et al.* (2000) say that there was 'no statistical relationship between the seriousness of carer shortages experienced and the frequency of local-authority recruitment patterns'. What determined the type and frequency of campaigns was the budget. This also affected who was available to answer questions, visit respondents and carry out assessment and preparatory work.

A commonly understood fact about recruitment is that word of mouth is the most significant single way that foster carers come to the service. When Triseliotis *et al.* (2000) asked how carers found out about fostering, of the 889 surveyed, most (413 or 46 per cent) cited friends, relatives, through work or that they 'always knew'. This confirmed the belief in the efficacy of personal contact noted by Triseliotis *et al.* (1995b). One hundred and sixty nine carers (19 per cent) learned about fostering opportunities through a newspaper article and only a few less (148 or 17 per cent) through a newspaper advertisement. Television and radio informed 97 (11 per cent), 26 were approached by the department (3 per cent), and 'other' ways of finding out attracted 36 (4 per cent).

Of course, there is the other side to the coin whereby foster carers are actually the best recruiters. When they gain satisfaction from what they do and are well remunerated and supported, they recommend it to others. However, if they feel they are being exploited or unsupported, they won't give a picture that will attract their friends, relatives and neighbours.

The Social Care Institute for Excellence (2004) confirms that word of mouth is one of the most successful ways in which foster carers come into the service but it also says that local newspaper articles are effective, as well as 'a consistently high local profile'. Thus, we can infer that the opposite – one-off, unsystematic campaigns are less effective because 'on-going publicity' achieves more.

A high profile is important, as a Scottish study (Triseliotis *et al.* 1995b), that made reference to England, showed. The same study emphasized that while a pitch that implied that 'anyone can foster' is unhelpful, there was not enough emphasis on the professionalism of the task, the possibilities of training and of obtaining qualifications, and status, and the financial rewards.

Recruitment is a problem in all the countries of the UK, though within each some areas fare better than others. One voluntary agency in Northern Ireland placed a newspaper advertisement that recruited one person and one couple turned up at an information meeting. The four health and social services trusts in the province took a joint advertisement in order to target people over 40. No one came forward (Personal information).

However, once in the service, it does not seem that it is, primarily, pay that causes people, from whatever background, to leave – even though in our society what we are paid is an indicator of the value placed upon us. The most common findings from research back up the anecdotal evidence, which is (as Bebbington and Miles (1990) put it) feeling 'undervalued and unsupported'. When a child leaves a carer, it costs nothing for the local authority to write a letter of appreciation and to acknowledge achievement but it will mean a great deal to the carer but this rarely happens.

Low status, lack of recognition, not being treated as a part of a team, lack of social-work support, being put upon – this is too often the daily lot of foster carers, which they have to balance against the satisfactions of the task. Certainly, these, too, are the negative feelings that have caused some carers to go from children's services departments to independent agencies, where, evidence suggests, the value of the good foster carer is realized in a practical way. Triseliotis *et al.* (2000) found that the lowest recruitment occurred mainly in authorities where carers 'disagreed' or 'disagreed strongly' that their social worker was available when needed.

Foster carers may also leave because they feel that they have done the work for too long. This is where local authorities need to be creative – if a foster carer feels no longer able to do the frontline work (either permanently or seeking only temporary respite) it would be tragic if that expertise were to be lost. These people could be used to train new foster carers or – as they do in Edinburgh – to work as classroom assistants in schools where there are fostered children. Foster carers also have other skills: some have been in social work, nursing, or training. All these could be used for the good of the service.

So far as recruitment and remuneration are concerned, independent fostering agencies tend to pay more, while local authority systems are far from straightforward and rates vary greatly. Some councils pay even less than the Fostering Network-recommended minimum; some pay fees; some make payments for assessed levels of skills and training. Neighbouring authorities may pay very different rates. Such inconsistency itself would seem to prove the central complaint of foster carers – that they are undervalued, taken for granted and have low status.

This should hardly be surprising. Lingering around fostering is its long history of being considered something that people should not be paid to do (see Triseliotis *et al.* 1995b). It was, after all, only in 1983 that adoption allowances were introduced. Denmark has paid foster carers a salary since 1970. Triseliotis *et al.* (2000) found that recruitment campaigns failed to say much about money which, to them, suggested that caring and financial reward were not thought of as going together. It is often luck of the draw how foster carers are paid by their local authorities: some get a fee and an allowance, some only get an allowance. In 2006, 60 per cent of foster carers in the UK received a fee, while 40 per cent did not. Seventy-five per cent earned less than the National Minimum Wage and 77 per cent earned less than £200 a week (Swain 2007).

At present foster-care tax relief doesn't explicitly differentiate between fees and allowances, although the way it is set up (a £10,000 annual exemption plus £200 per week for children under 11 or £250 for those over 11) may give scope to do so in the future. Currently a fostering couple are assessed together for tax purposes. At the present time very few foster carers exceed these thresholds but it is believed that the number who do is rising due to both increased allowances and an increasing number of fostering services paying fees.

Fostering Network has campaigned for a national payment structure that pays foster carers for their work and skills. Such a structure would also include realistic retainers between placements because many foster carers only receive payment when a child is placed with them, so they also experience financial hardship when there are gaps between children staying with them.

Unless foster care is to be converted to a full- or part-time salaried job, which has its disadvantages, it needs flexibility in its remuneration. This should not be the kind of flexibility we have at the moment, which is one that entails inconsistency. Rather, there should be guaranteed reasonable minimum fees that also allow for payment for skills and recognize the difficulties and complexity of the job, and do not allow for discrimination against carers in the benefits and tax system. Such flexibility would not only afford foster carers fairness but it would also suit the different needs of the variety of people who are foster carers.

If foster care is to meet the present shortage of placements, there needs to be a major change in how it is seen, as we go on to discuss with regard to professionalism (see below). This is a two-way street, where increased demands need to be met by increased status, acceptance and rewards underpinned by a clear set of values and a knowledge base. This would allow foster carers' employment status to acquire a sounder basis and allow them a clear career progression. National registration would be both a part of enhanced status and allow foster carers greater freedom of movement as to where they practised (see below).

In addition to recruiting and retaining carers, attention needs to be given to the reasons why people decide *not* to become carers. Some arguments for this are advanced by Triseliotis *et al.* (2000), and they list them as follows:

- 'widespread ignorance' about child-care needs and fostering
- lack of confidence that people could do the job
- 'protracted assessments or fears about not measuring up to agency expectations and of being rejected resulting in shaming'
- mistrust of social workers on account of their lack of credibility and their 'perceived intrusiveness'
- the children's problems
- discomfort at the idea of returning children to their families
- lack of accommodation
- fears about false allegations of abuse.

The bright side of the coin shows that:

- overwhelmingly foster carers have altruistic motives
- they believe they have something positive to give
- they have a commitment to disadvantaged children, and
- they have 'a heightened sense of the awareness about child care need' (Triseliotis *et al.* 2000).

These authors also discovered that carers who were single were 'more likely to say that they had "never" thought of giving up fostering and that fostering met with their expectations wholly or partly'.

Perhaps the most significant conclusion is the one reached by Sinclair and colleagues (2004):

> The most important and impressive feature of fostering is probably the commitment of the foster carers. (p.155)

Foster carers need a status that reflects their standing within the child-care team. They will only come forward and stay in the service once recruited if they can see, in practical ways (financial and otherwise), what we mean when we talk about valuing fostering and those who provide it

Toward a professional service

The most significant advance after foster care was statutorily recognized 40 years before came in the 1970s when Nancy Hazel established the Kent Family Placement Project. (Hazel 1981). The scheme had a number of experimental elements and was based on other ideas current at the time, like normalization and community care, which were having their impact on services like those for people with a learning disability and people with mental-health problems. The key features of the Kent scheme included a belief that even difficult teenagers (it was aimed at this age group) could be cared for within the community. Foster carers were to be trained, young people were to be prepared before placement, and there was to be provision of support after placement for both foster carers and the young people. But not the least far-reaching innovation was the creation of a fee-based service. This marked the advent of 'professional fostering'.

In the 30 years since the scheme was established, its principles have become standard practice in local authorities, voluntary bodies and independent fostering agencies. However, the professionalization of fostering through the payment of reward has continued to be debated. This is because payment brings into focus questions of the status of fostering and those who provide it – are they fellow professionals? One may be paid to do the job – in this case, looking after children – but what is the motive of the carer? Is fostering a voluntary and philanthropic activity? Should it be rewarded? Can someone be paid to have a relationship with a child?

These are not easy questions to answer, and to argue for or against them itself raises many more questions about the nature and shape of fostering services; the relationship between carers and social workers; and the issues around the approval and status of foster carers. All of these are highlighted by the introduction of Children's Workforce Development Council standards for foster care in 2008, which make foster carers the only non-salaried group subject to such standards.

Kirton, Beecham and Ogilvie (2007) found that carers' sense of being valued was linked to a wide range of factors about them as individuals, as well as whether they were regarded by others (such as social workers) as colleagues, 'clients' or something in between. Until this fundamental question about status and standing is resolved, it is unlikely that foster care can meet the hopes and expectations of the other partners in the system: social workers; parents; children; and other professionals.

For foster carers to be seen as acting professionally (which is not necessarily the same as being a member of a profession), they have to be recognized as such by all of their partners. This will be helped if foster carers:

- have a formal qualification, which is subject to independent verification

- have a national registration system; and

- develop a knowledge base and/or (like social work) adapt the knowledge base of others – like, for example, child psychology – in order to suit their needs.

Knowledge about fostering is growing, based, in part, on the now fairly well-established and increasing research about it. It is arguable, though, whether or not fostering has a knowledge base peculiar to itself or whether, like social work, it draws from the knowledge base of other professional groups like, for example, psychology. For the foster carer, a national recognition award might be comparable to, for example, the postgraduate certificate in education, or membership of the Association of Certified Chartered Accountants or the Institute of Cost and Management Accountants.

The standards developed by the Children's Workforce Development Council, their links to the NVQ3 in child care, and the emergence of a foundation degree in therapeutic care open to foster carers are a starting point, but as yet there is no clear overall framework of qualifications. This is urgently needed, particularly as some children being placed with carers are more and more challenging, have more complex problems and needs, have suffered trauma, and require a clear framework for work. There should not be an assumption that such children can be placed immediately with a family. This does not mean that they will *not* be placed with a family but rather that what is needed is a proper assessment of the child, the family and the impact of the child upon the family before they are placed.

Currently, foster carers are approved by local fostering panels based in local authorities, voluntary child-care agencies, or independent fostering agencies. A foster carer who wishes to work elsewhere – with another agency or in another local authority area – has to resign as a carer from one local authority and then be re-assessed and re-approved by another. Compare this with the situation for teachers, social workers, doctors and nurses (as well as other professionals, like accountants and architects) who are registered with a national regulator, which allows their registration to be portable.

The Green Paper, *Care Matters* (Department for Education and Skills 2006) proposed that foster carers should be registered, like the others in social care with whom they work, with the General Social Care Council. However, this did not find its way into the Children and Young Persons Act that was going through Parliament at the time of writing.

Such changes to the foster care service would allow it to develop professionally. It would be supported by standards of practice that could address the issues of placement stability, placement choice, appropriate record keeping, and continuous professional development, and national registration.

A high-quality professional fostering service is one that recognizes:

- the importance of the child
- the true cost of fostering
- the value of the carer
- the importance of the child's parents; and
- the need for training and continuous professional development.

Research by Berridge (2005) has shown that:

Overall, carers should feel part of a team. Whatever its other merits, training for foster carers had no simple, direct link with improved child-care outcomes. The studies [on which Berridge draws] did not provide evidence that any particular organizational structure for fostering services produced better outcomes. (p.8)

So, while all the main issues that we have discussed here are important, perhaps the most important is that carers should feel valued members of the team.

Preparation and training

During the 1960s and 1970s, the assessment of carers began to look at the ability of the carers but only in the context of the most difficult situations and behaviours they were likely to meet and how they might cope with them. Since then there has been an increased focus on the recruitment, assessment, training and preparation of carers because the past 30 years have seen many changes in foster care. This is due not least to the fact that as more and more children have been considered for fostering, so children being placed are more and more challenging. Once, certain children were regarded as being unfosterable. However, the work of Hazel (1981), much subsequent British practice and the Oregon Multidimensional Treatment Foster Scheme (Chamberlain 2003) – which is now being developed in England (National Implementation Team 2007) – has shown that this is not the case.

Fostering has come to be seen in the past two decades as not just about looking after children and, as such, requiring a more professional approach to assessment and training. As a result of such a realization, assessment has been developed that looks at carer histories and also carers' ability to understand and complete the task.

The competency-based model, which has been fashionable in the past few years, looks at what carers already do. Both Fostering Network and BAAF Adoption and Fostering produce competency assessment lists, and the acknowledged qualification for carers is the NVQ, a competency-based qualification. The standards for foster carers issued by the Children's Workforce Development Council are also based on competencies, and their development of knowledge and expertise.

However, as Chris Dare once said: 'It is not what children do, but what they make you feel that decides if a placement endures.' As we have described in Chapter 1, feelings are a major factor in fostering, and it is for this reason that understanding carers' own lives is important in enabling them to reflect on their lives, the feelings evoked and what brings them to fostering. For traumatized children it is particularly important that carers understand their own feelings, as children will bring to them powerful feelings and emotions because of the trauma and abuse they have suffered. Such feelings will resonate with carers, and can generate equally powerful feelings and emotions in others of revulsion, horror, protectiveness.

It is, therefore, very important that carers should know themselves, have a strong sense of identity and be resilient. The impact that caring for a traumatized child can have on a family is acknowledged by the recent recognition of the possibility of symptoms similar to post-traumatic stress disorder appearing in foster carers. As Kunstal (1998) has written: 'When a family takes on an emotionally injured, challenging child – especially if that child is older...they, in a sense, are also importing the child's pathology.' He goes on to say:

> Remember that you will be influenced more by these children than they will by you. These unfortunate and challenging children often have the power and ability to find and exploit your emotional Achilles' Heel. At a time when you must parent to your best, these children often succeed in bringing out your parenting at its worst. (p.2)

We also know that it is important that the interlinked matters of emotions and emotional responses are explored within fostering. If they are not, then these issues can be acted out by the parent and their anger and frustration can then lead to concerns about child protection. Such responses need to be covered in supervision where support can be given to carers. It is often difficult to talk about the closeness and intimacy of the work of carers, and the starting point for this is in the assessment process.

The assessment process

Guishard-Pine, McCall and Hamilton (2007) comment:

> The assessor will also inform you [the foster carer] about the 'preparation groups' that have an important role in letting you know about all what fostering involves. There is usually a series of meetings over several weeks that you are expected to attend. They will run both in the daytime and also in the evenings to accommodate people who are working full-time. You will get a chance to meet other people who are interested in fostering, and you will also be able to meet experienced

foster carers and specialists in child development and child care. Your attendance and contribution may form part of our assessment. After this series of meetings you will usually be asked to think, together with your family and/or your support network, about whether you should go on to the next stage of the assessment. (pp.145–148)

However, fostering preparation courses cannot cover all areas that may arise, so it's important that they are thought provoking and provide both an opportunity for information sharing and a chance to explore issues that occur to potential carers during the course.

As fostering is, in the main, an occupation requiring 24 hour involvement, it is worth considering how best to give people a taste of the intensity of that experience. A weekend residential course meets the needs of training and assessment, which should be a key part of recruitment. However, if run in a certain way it can also model something of the intensity of the experience of fostering.

All applicants for foster caring and their families should be visited at their home once, if not twice, and potential carers should be given an opportunity to discuss with the family-placement team how their application will progress. If applicants choose to continue with the process then the whole family should be invited to a residential weekend.

A programme for residential training

The programme offered by SACCS at such a weekend is the first of a set of building blocks of training (as illustrated in Figure 3.1). It is followed later by:

- initial training about the recovery programme
- training about attachment
- further fostering training
- the foundation degree in therapeutic child care; and
- child-specific training.

The SACCS weekend covers aspects of fostering including:

- child development
- the affects of abuse

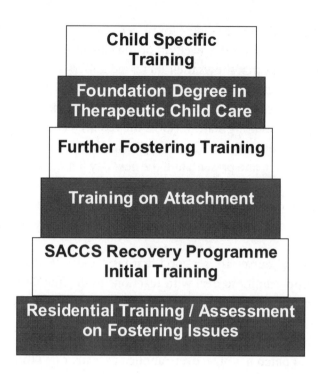

Figure 3.1 The building blocks of training

- attachment and separation
- the role of a foster carer
- managing behaviour, and
- safe caring.

The courses are a mixture of small and large group work, case study and experiential learning. The weekend starts on Friday with tea, and finishes on Sunday afternoon. It is a very intensive and exhausting experience, but, as such, reflects what fostering feels like. It is intended to model good experiences of foster care. For example, the anxiety that may be evoked in carers coming to an unfamiliar venue can help them understand how children can feel when moving into placement.

Prior to the course applicants can discuss what they feel they need to resolve in order to attend – for example, in order to be thoroughly prepared, just as children should be for placement. At this time, too, as well as on the Friday and Saturday evening of the course, participants are also expected to do work that shows their increased understanding of fostering and its likely impact on their families.

The weekend uses in-house material for foster carers as well as that used with therapeutic parenting staff. It fulfils the requirements of the National Minimum Standards of Foster Care. Course work is to be done on Friday night for preparation and presentation the next day. This is also done on the Saturday night for presentation on Sunday. This writing, together with doing contemporaneous work, reflects the future requirements of carers to write diary sheets and make written records or diaries – a key skill for foster carers.

While such a course offers a good first taste, a day held a month later provides an opportunity to deal with reactions to the initial weekend and the chance to concentrate on other issues, as well as develop those already discussed.

The training on recovery and assessment is a five-day course, which includes the 24 outcomes of recovery applied to foster care (Tomlinson and Philpot 2008).

A session on attachment offers further intensive training and is linked to the integration of care and therapy, so that carers understand that the therapeutic parenting approach, which they will adopt, involves not only care but also therapeutic understanding – which leads to 'therapeutic parenting', which, as explained above, is different from just parenting. It is this that makes fostering different from parenting.

Further fostering training is also offered in a range of courses looking at aspects of fostering discussed in the residential course but now taken further, with concentration on:

- safe caring
- managing allegations against the carer
- independent support
- contact with the birth family
- behaviour management
- moving on from placement

- education
- self-esteem and identity; and
- first aid.

The foundation degree in therapeutic child care is organized through the Mary Walsh Institute with Glyndwr University. It has ten modules covering:

- induction to the work and initial foundation training on the work required and responsibilities of the job
- the 24 recovery outcomes
- developing knowledge and practice
- child development
- attachment, grief and loss
- social development and communication
- understanding and developing emotional intelligence
- identity and diversity
- sexual development and sexuality; and
- critical professional and personal development done with a reflective journal.

Also available is child-specific training, which is concerned with that which arises from the specific needs of an individual child. This may include matters concerning disability, particular interests, or particular consequences of the trauma that the child has suffered.

CHAPTER 4

Fostering, Loss and Opportunity

The child who comes into foster care is a child who has suffered loss: the loss of family, home, school and school friends. Indeed, it is also a loss of the small everyday details in an environment, which may be unnoticed at the time: its smells, sights and familiarities. Many of those things that the child has lost may not be positive – what members of the family may have done to her, the sounds and noises associated with bad experiences – but they will still all be part of the loss of the familiar. And we are grounded in the familiar: it helps us to know who we are and our place in the world. This is a grounding that so many abused children lack and the small part which they may have acquired is just that part that the move to fostering, a new environment, will take from them.

So, even a child who wants to leave the place in which she finds herself may leave behind positive things. A child moving into fostering from residential care may feel that she is relinquishing things like safety, security, attachment and containment. Children who do not resist a move can show a superficial acceptance but they may also show signs of an attachment disorder or an ambivalent attachment. Thus, when a child shows no emotion this is not a good sign – it may mask how they are *really* feeling and their ambivalence.

This loss is not one way – a foster carer may also suffer a sense of loss. If her own children have left home – and research shows that foster carers are more likely not to have children at home than those who do not foster – then she may feel a sense of loss of purpose, of children to care for. This may be one of the reasons why she has become a foster carer; indeed, the fact that she is wanting to offer to do so can imply that she senses this gap. As a foster carer she may suffer another kind of loss – that gap which falls between what she had expected of her calling and its reality. This is not to say that fostering is not satisfying and rewarding; but few things are wholly unblemished, few dreams are ever wholly realized. Fostering will also meet a need in the carer: no altruism is ever pure and the foster carer, like others, will hope for some return, something back in the relationship with the child. A child may well reveal to the carer, the carer's own losses.

Losses will be specific to each individual and these are only some of the losses that can affect the two most important people with whom this book is concerned – the foster carer and the foster child – but loss is a part of life. It is something which we all suffer and have to learn to deal with:

- the sense sometimes that the past was better but that one cannot step back in time

- the death of loved ones

- the loss occasioned by opportunities not taken, aspirations not reached

- the loss of a loved and familiar place when a house move is unavoidable

- the loss of a job that can lead to a feeling of purposeless

- the loss involved in a relationship breakdown

- the loss not only when children grow up and become independent but also when, as sometimes happens, they move a good distance from home; and,

- with age, the loss of faculties – which makes us start to recognize the ageing process.

Few losses are replaceable. There is usually little chance of regaining what has gone. Loss creates a gap that cannot be crossed, a void that cannot be filled by what has gone, but it can also present an opportunity for something new to emerge – like, for example, the new interest in fostering. How well we manage losses, cope with them, adjust to them, and come to accept them is a sign of our emotional maturity. It is, then, one of the important roles of the foster carer to help the child come to terms with, and understand, not just *what* she has lost but the fact that those losses are part of a wider cycle of loss. In this there are parallels with the continuum of grief that Kübler-Ross (1970) posits about dying. The person who is dying, she says, goes through five stages: denial and isolation; anger; bargaining; depression and acceptance. If we take these as applying to loss generally, we can see that there is nothing unusual about this. This process doesn't just apply to some people: everyone has to go through this cycle when they lose something – and an abused child, a child in care, is no exception.

Perhaps one of the most irreplaceable losses of all is that which is felt by a parent – losing a child. When a child is placed with foster carers – and certainly when a child is adopted – this can be a final confirmation to a parent that the child or children will not be returning home. The parents hope was that once the child was 'cured' she could come back. Loss felt by parents can produce intense relationships between them, carers and children. The sense of their own 'badness' which parents can feel, or a sense of their not being good enough and the associated feelings, are passed around between members of the family placement team, and this can produce stress and placement disruption (see below).

The losses that an abused child may experience may evoke strong feelings of the past and will put pressure on her newly acquired and embedded inner working model.

The internal working model

An understanding of loss (as well as other experiences) in children is critical to appreciating how this affects their internal working model. Children develop four kinds of internal working model that lead to different kinds of attachments, which are described as follows:

- secure (the carer is loving and the child is loved)

- ambivalent (the caregiver is inconsistent in how he responds and the child sees herself as dependant and poorly valued)

- avoidant (the caregiver is seen as consistently rejecting and the child is insecure but compulsively self-reliant); or

- disorganized (caregivers are seen as frightening or frightened and the child is helpless, or angry and controlling) (Howe 2000).

The last response is one often associated with children who have been abused and the third model – avoidant – can be observed in children who have undergone multiple placements (see Chapter 2).

Archer (2003) calls internal working models 'road maps' providing the child with an internal framework of her world. This framework, according to Burnell and Archer (2003):

> maps out the most suitable response-routes to familiar, and unfamiliar challenges, IWMs [internal working models] reflect the child's view of, and confidence in, the attachment figures' capacity to provide a safe and caring environment. Moreover, these models, in turn, organize the child's thoughts, memories and feelings regarding attachment figures. Inevitably, they will also act as guides and predictors of future behavior for the child and analogous attachment figures, such as adoptive parents. (p.65)

Schore (1994) says that these models are burned into the unconscious at the neurobiological level and Solomon and George (1996) believe that, once established, they are highly resistant to change as they have different experiences.

The essential thing about loss is that its effects can extend from the original object that is lost – say, the parent – to the foster carer, social worker, friends and family. Children can also become disengaged from school and the community. Those who experience a number of placements in care can undergo a triple loss – of a sense of belonging, of individuals and of place because they may be situated hundreds of miles from their original home, community and family.

Working with loss

Loss can inhibit a child's ability to use the relationships and healthy environment made available to them. To better understand the child, and to find the key way through this, it is helpful to adapt Kübler-Ross's (1970) stages of the understanding of the grieving process to the following:

- shock

- anger
- despair, adjustment
- moving forward.

An abused child must move through these stages, just as the dying person moves through the stages proposed by Kübler-Ross (1970). She cannot skip them or avoid them but she must not get stuck at one of them. What the foster carer cannot do is try to compensate or make up for the losses (in the way that a child who loses one toy can be given another). To attempt to do that will only prevent and thus repress (with all the consequences which that would entail) the necessary movement forward. It is, therefore, the foster carer's job to help the child through that cycle, along that journey. The foster carer may have suffered her own losses but she is not like the child in that she has probably adjusted to her losses, has understood them, and will have the maturity to relate her own experience of loss to what the child is going through. Children, especially those who have been abused, do not have this insight or the empathy to relate their losses to those of other people. The gifts of her own insight, maturity and empathy are what the foster carer can bring to the child. Here the foster carer is like a parent but she is also like a therapist; she offers not just parenting but therapeutic parenting (Pughe and Philpot 2007). She therefore needs not only to understand how the child is reacting to her loss but what the child's trigger points are.

It is dangerous to start from what may be the most obvious – love – because children who have been abused have learned to distrust love and intimacy because these have been misused by those who have abused them. The foster carer must also beware of offering responses to a child which, in other circumstances, would be unexceptional. For example, she must be careful in her response to the child's anger in order to calm the child and the situation. The foster carer's own sense of loss through failure to succeed may start a negative cycle which can be seen as punitive or even abusive. In such a case, the foster carer needs to be able to step back, reflect, and gain support and knowledge through supervision and consultancy, so that her emotions do not predominate in her reactions.

One aspect of helping the child come to understand loss is to help her see that her life is now different and what that entails – that her internal working model has, for example, moved from a sense of worthlessness to one of value, from her being afraid to feeling safe. We could see this realization on the child's part as taking her through a hierarchy, akin to that 'hierarchy of needs' formulated by Maslow (1954). (see Rose and Philpot 2008, pps 21–22)

Children who have been abused are familiar with anger and aggression in families and are often, in fact, uncomfortable with regard, warmth and compliments. For example, a carer may say that a child looks pretty, that she is attractively dressed or that her hair looks nice. The child may respond by cutting her hair, tearing her clothes or making herself look unattractive. In this way she puts herself back into the shadow of abuse. She is not used to compliments and doesn't feel worthy of them. Compliments, too, may have been a prelude to abuse. If the child is uncomfortable with the positive feelings and attitudes expressed by the foster carer, the carer can then feel rejected, and can react with anger and feel upset (after all, hasn't she become a foster carer in order to offer something, to help?). In the child's eyes this, then, invalidates what the carer has said, expressed and is trying to do. It is especially hard for a foster carer if this happens when the child has been in her care for a considerable period of time, when she may believe that negative behaviour has diminished. The foster carer can then feel that she has failed.

However, such behaviour has to be seen in relation to key steps in the stages of development in a fostering placement, which are:

- honeymoon and moving in
- distancing from the family
- challenging the foster family
- adjustment.

In each of these phases or steps there are tasks that need to be done, so that children can make successful transitions. Foster carers need to remember that they are not responsible for children's pasts, and that they cannot compensate them for that. However, foster carers can continue to support children, and help them face their pain and continue to make sense of it. In this way they will be continuing to help children embed a new internalized working model and will be continuing the process of therapeutic parenting.

The tasks for each step are as follows.

Shock/honeymoon The honeymoon phase will follow even the best introductions phase (see Chapter 6). It can seem that there has been a seamless transition, because the child may appear unaffected, or be unusually happy. At this time it is important that the carer continues the process of making the child feel welcome, and of encouraging positive friendships within the home, school and community. A key part of this process will be not being afraid to say 'no', and being able to establish boundaries and guidelines so that the safety and containment provided previously is continued. It is important not to be seduced by behaviour that is almost too good to be true. Carers will want to see behaviour as positive, but they may lose sight of the way that shock can produce such behaviour, and how important it is to recognize that children need to talk to them about the loss as part of the process of resolution. Just as we would be worried for a grieving person who sought to deny his past and his past relationships, we should be worried by children who show no emotional reactions to moves – in fact, we should be just as worried as if they were acting out. No reaction in a child is not a sign that everything is going well, it could be a shock reaction. The child could either be in shock or be lacking any capacity to attach. Indeed, some carers would say that the honeymoon period had never actually begun and that the child has gone into freeze, flight and fight as a response to the trauma of the move.

Anger/distancing In this stage, the reality of the situation will be beginning to hit home, and there will be feelings of anger and confusion. This anger can be directed at those who in the past are perceived to have let the child down, or whom it is safer for the child to target. Often it is foster carers who become the victim of anger, and the degree of anger seems disproportionate to the event that is the trigger. During this period it is important that the carer shows patience and perseverance, and keeps to established routines and boundaries. It will be a period of testing out for the carer that he can withstand the child's feelings and contain them.

It is often easy, but is actually wrong, to become overprotective. There is a need for understanding and management of the anger in the same way that the anger is centred within the therapeutic parenting model in residential care. At these times the child will need to feel safely managed and supported, and to have an acknowledgement of their pain and distress. This often offers a chance to revisit past understanding, through life-story work. The child's need will be for the foster carer to stay alongside her but at a safe distance, and this is a more productive way forward than trying to keep the child busy to keep her mind off things, although physical activity can have a place in breaking a negative cycle. The key then, is not to divert or hurry the child through the process of grieving, but to actively encourage her to think about her losses, allowing her to engage and talk about them. This is about remembering both sad and happy times.

Despair/challenging After anger can come despair when the child physically withdraws from and avoids engaging with the family. There may be occasional outbursts of anger, and carers have been hit by children, often followed by foster carers feeling that the child just doesn't care. This can be a very unrewarding part of fostering and lead to the carer feeling useless, that they are not helping and are being rejected, and that they would be better off seeking to help someone who does want help. It is often at this stage that placements can be put under real pressure and break down because the reality is not congruent with the carer's hopes and expectations.

Furthermore, as carers work with children in this stage of the grieving process, their own wounds and losses can be opened, thus producing a heady cocktail. It is important that carers receive supervision and consultancy at this time so that they can differentiate between their feelings and those of the child, and the feelings that the child has given to them. At this time carers have to be strong, and to recognize their own experiences, so that their defences do not stop them helping the child because of the overwhelming need to protect themselves. It is easy to become rejecting at this stage.

It is important in this phase to play the 'emotional detective' (Kunstal 1998) and use the information provided about the child to begin to work out what is happening, and what events and feelings are being re-lived. This is information which can come from others who have worked with the child. In this way carers will feel empowered and be able to recognize that what is happening is not about them. This will enable them to adopt a therapeutic parenting approach of

- being sensitive

- backing off where appropriate; and

- offering the child a sense of safety and containment that comes from recognition of their pain.

It is important that carers are willing and able to identify to the child their emotional needs and feelings and then work with the child on them.

Adjustment / acceptance This is the beginning of the process of acceptance which, in time, becomes attachment – that is, when the child can be seen overall as being more settled, with a growing sense of contentment and self-confidence. Issues and triggers will still arise, but the child's reaction will be characterized by an ability (often supplied by their carers) to pull themselves back, and then moving on to appropriate understanding. The feelings will not have gone away. These can be shock, anger and despair, which may trigger special reactions, but the child is able to recognize these feelings and seek appropriate help.

There is no formula for a timescale for this process of adjustment to occur. How long does it take to overcome trauma? How long might a child need in order to overcome past difficulties and problems? On occasions, long-term fostering can seem painfully slow, but the passage of time helps with this process and foster care here is about undoing before re-parenting. Although undoing can be done in residential care and children are then ready for re-parenting, being placed in a family will immediately challenge that. However this will be an issue that has been challenged with the child previously, and the process of change and accepting re-parenting may be able to be accepted more readily.

The tasks for carers in the adjustment are many and various. There is a tendency on occasion to react ahead to progress and remove the boundaries that have provided safety or containment. But there is a reason for plans to remain in place, with small changes as appropriate and for a period of consolidation and acceptance to happen. It is also important to acknowledge to children that it is permissible to make a mistake and that these will not be held against them or brought up again.

It is important to recognize that going through this process of development in a fostering placement may be different in children at different stages in life and is not necessarily linear. Sometimes just as things are looking good, issues may arise. The child may then need to return to some issues to reassure herself, and there may also be outside trigger points that mean that the issues resurface. This is not a sign of failure.

The pattern of resolution of feelings will vary from child to child. Some children show no anger response, but move quickly to despair and seem to become 'stuck' there. Others seem to become 'stuck' in anger and have trouble moving to subsequent stages. Adjustment involves dealing both with feelings of anger and feelings of despair. Furthermore, moving a child in the middle of a stage runs a great risk of the child then being stuck at that stage and needing special help to get through it.

Foster care, the past and reality

The grief process for some children involves grieving for a parent–child relationship that never occurred. Their grief here is about not having had a parent who was able to love and care for them continuously. This form of grieving carries just as much emotional pain as other kinds but frequently there is less support for it. The best start in life is to be born to parents who love you and are capable of caring for you until you are mature enough to care for yourself. That is the natural order of things. It is what most children can take for granted, but children who come into foster care do not have this support. They hurt. They know something is missing, that something is wrong. Too many children who come into foster care are in pain.

Whenever we lose someone or something that is important to us, we suffer from the loss. Divorce, the death of someone close, the end of a valued relationship – all these bring intense suffering and can create feelings of loneliness, rejection, anger and guilt, as well as wondering about how things could have been done differently. A preoccupation with one's own thoughts can interfere with one's ability to get on with the tasks to hand and create irritability with others. It can take a long time before one is able to treat the world in a normal way. Such suffering is great and often incomprehensible for adults. How much more so, then, for children, who are vulnerable and may have to lose what they depend on. Given the number of losses piled on them, it is astonishing that children are able to adjust at all. Some, of course, never do.

Foster carers cannot bear the responsibility for children's problems but there are things they can do that can help children face their pain, understand it and move forward, and (by doing what is described above) to help them through the grieving process. A task that continues throughout the fostering placement is that of recognizing the severity of the child's pain. This is not easy. We do not like to see children in pain. In fact, one of the most important reasons why people come forward to be selected as foster parents is precisely because they do not want children to suffer. Love and comfort will help but therapeutic parents are expected to do more. Giving true comfort and enabling recovery cannot be accomplished by pretending there is no pain. It can be accomplished by the foster carer letting the child know that she and her past are understood.

No matter how miserable the past, it is never totally negative, and children may cling to the very slightest evidence that they were treated well. And why shouldn't they? It can be difficult sometimes to understand how children can idealize relationships that are known to have been far from ideal. However, sometimes it is even more difficult to hear children berate their parents. We do not like to think about parents' cruelty to children, but if the children are not allowed to talk about their ambivalent feelings, they will never come to understand themselves. If they are led to believe these very normal feelings should be hidden, they will feel that something is wrong with them, and their self-esteem will suffer.

Children should be encouraged to speak freely, and foster parents should not be judgemental. There is no need to justify the birth parents' undesirable behaviour. There is a need to let the children know it is normal for them to have mixed feelings about themselves and their parents. When they know their feelings are acceptable, they can begin to sort them out. This is a very slow process and one that needs to be repeated again and again.

To accept a child's feelings, is to accept the child. When a child is accepted, she is helped to accept herself. That is the basis of personal growth in recovery.

Questions

- Think of a major loss which you have experienced. How did you come to terms with it? Think of a similar loss suffered by someone you know and consider if they dealt with it differently and how.

- Think of a major loss which someone you know has sustained. Were you able to help them? If so, how? If not, why?

- Think of a comparatively trivial loss but one which affected you deeply. Why was that?

- Can you think of three losses that all children experience and three which only a child in care experiences?

- Think of a child you have placed where the placement seemed to be working well and then matters changed. What changed and what were the reactions to that?

Loss and placement

When we discuss and think about loss, we must also remember that it is something that also applies to all those involved in the process of placing a child. The impact of a child moving on the other people in the family placement team, both closer and further afield, should not be underestimated.

We have referred above to the sense of loss that parents can feel and how this can negatively influence the team. For foster carers, placement can be seen as achieving a goal that people wanted to achieve. But at the point of the placement, there are also concerns and worries about whether they will be good enough; whether the child will like them; and what would happen if they fail.

All carers' sense of self can be challenged at times and this is true even for the most experienced carer. It is important that any feelings of loss of status and reputation are acknowledged and worked with. At the point of placement, the carers' reputation, along with that of the assessing social worker and the child's social worker, could suffer if the placement fails.

For residential workers, the point of placement can also be difficult when the child to whom they have formed an attachment moves on. There is, therefore, a considerable sense of loss, anxiety and concern. It is important for all the parties concerned in fostering that the losses at any particular point are acknowledged in supervision.

Question

- List the losses for the individual members of the family placement team in the last placement in which you were involved. What behaviour might result from such losses and did you see this happen or experience it yourself, during the placement?

CHAPTER 5

Practising to Make Perfect: Introductions and the Practice Family

Introductions: the importance of getting things right

The process of introductions includes all the general discussion with the child about placement, as well as specific discussion about a family and then the practical details of introduction including sharing information, visits and education. When a child has emerged from the intense work of therapy, life story and therapeutic parenting her progress will be assessed and a judgement made about whether she is ready yet to benefit from a long-term family placement. This is a critical juncture in her journey to recovery and the process of introductions, therefore, not only involves the actual process, but builds on the work done in the period prior to this. It is the key factor in building the firm foundations of a successful placement. In the introductory process, the child and her needs should be at the centre of everything the team is doing. The overall aim of the placement is to promote the well-being of the child and to help her develop successfully. Moving to a new foster family can be a difficult and wearying process for these children. Some of them may have had the experience of a practice family but being in a family full time is very different from part time.

Any good placement philosophy should be based on:

- the recovery and assessment process indicating that the time for moving to a family is within the next 12 to 15 months

- the local authority that is responsible for the child being aware of, and in agreement with, the plan

- all members of the team being in agreement with the plan; and

- carers being seen as fellow professional colleagues, offering a continuation of the recovery programme from a family setting.

Identifying a new family will involve all the individual members of the foster team. This comprises:

- the children's services department

- the residential home

- the family-placement service of the agency where the child is cared for

- the therapy, therapeutic parenting and life-story work team; and

- (where appropriate) the practice family.

These, in many senses, surround the child and focus on her. During the whole process of planning the move through to introductions and the move actually taking place, the team will meet regularly. These meetings will be critical in establishing the feel and pace of the placement. It is important that all parties are committed to the process and are able to offer an understanding of the child from their own perspective.

Children and young people who have made good progress toward recovery and whose progress is continuing would be considered as being likely for a family placement within the next 15 months. After consultation with the therapeutic parenting team, and the home and staff, and, if they are in agreement, a member of the family-placement team will be allocated to that child. For the first three months, the social worker from the family-placement team will review the information held on the child. This will include:

- consultation with the residential care staff and the local authority

- reading the child's case file and the life-story file

- consultation with the life-story worker

- reading the child's therapy file

- consultation with the therapist

- reading the recovery and assessment file; and

- attending the recovery and assessment review.

The assessment allows an understanding of how the child is likely to behave in a family. This must look beyond the simple shared interests of the family and the child to be placed with them (which is a positive criterion) to issues of the family's way of life and functioning. The problem with concentrating on 'interests' is that the rejection of all common interests is a very powerful way in which a child may challenge the placement very early on. This is because interests and hobbies may be superficial and are not part of the fabric of family life. Both child and carer's interests, something they once held in common, may change.

Such an assessment process creates a holistic picture of the child and her functioning, and begins a process of constructing an outline profile of the type of family required, with particular regard to where the potential family live and to educational concerns. It may be that current foster carers match what is required; otherwise advertising in a specific location may be needed. This is not, though, about advertising children. Even under assumed names they can recognize themselves and if no one comes forward, they then suffer further rejection. However, advertising for carers each week over, say, a year may create interest about fostering in the minds of readers.

Good quality assessments of the family will be required. Reports going to panel for approval need to be comprehensive and look beyond competencies to an understanding of how the family functions.

The next step of matching involves all members of the family placement team: staff in the home (particularly the child's key carer), life-story worker, therapist, family placement worker and social worker. There will be visits, discussions, and formal matching agreements about the appropriateness of the placement of a child with a family at panels. The family-placement social worker is there to answer the child's questions and work with her anxieties about fostering, of which there will be many. He has to reassure the child while she is in the transition period before the move takes place and to work with the staff and the child's key carer about the child's worries, fantasies, her ideal of a 'perfect family', and differences between that and the reality.

The reality of a move and the consequent feelings of loss can reopen the child's past worries and concerns. It may also generate strong feelings for members of the family placement team. This is when work looking at different perceptions and understandings and the impact of loss needs to be carried out with therapeutic parenting and family placement staff. At this time the local authority will be considering profiles of a family required and visiting some families.

Clearly, this is all very time-intensive work, and it needs to be focused wholly on the child, with all team members working together, and being aware of their own feelings about the move. For the key carer and others in the family placement team there will not only be feelings about loss and separation on their part but also the sense they will have about being judged by others and questions to themselves about whether their work was good enough. When a child moves on the key carer is effectively told that his work has gone far enough, which can lead to feelings of inadequacy. For the child and young person in a residential home receiving treatment, safety comes from people and structure. It is important, therefore, that in this transition period we provide safety through structures and clarity.

Often at this stage, there is a sense of idealism by children when they will talk about wanting a big house and lots of money. Yet staff close to the child are not immune from idealizing placements and, for example, may want her to go to a family where there are no other children. Going from a residential home with five children to a family where there may be only one other child is a big move so considerable work would need to be done with all staff in such an instance in distinguishing between their own feelings – of inadequacy or the fear that the family will not be able to look after the child as well as the staff member can – and those of the child. Quite small matters can be metaphors for larger ones and for all involved can carry great emotional weight. There will be both objective and subjective concerns relating to the process of separation.

Moving to placement

All the family placement team continue to work together, focusing on the child. There can be pressure to rush children from residential to foster care but this must be resisted. A rushed introduction, which creates too much momentum at the expense of control, is not helpful. When this is happening there is a need to reflect and to think through what needs to be done and is going to be done. Pughe and Philpot (2007) advise:

> An introduction lasting eight to 12 weeks allows appropriate endings, therapeutic closure and time for 'excitement' – a child's initial pleasure at the possibility of a 'forever' family – withdrawal, which is handled by the recovery team and resolution: leaving the old home and arriving in the new one. (p.128)

This is a time not only of being introduced to the new family. It is also a time when other things must be put away. It is 'goodbye' as well as 'hello'. This will involve the emotional transfer of attachment from the secure base of the residential home and therapeutic parenting team. As in attachment theory, the child is 'claimed', that is, by someone who wants her to belong to him. The child is moving in different ways:

- physically (by the recovery team, social worker, school, friends and family)

- emotionally (by herself and by feeling strong and confident)

- and therapeutically (by having closure of the current therapeutic process).

There is nothing spontaneous and unplanned about any of this. The recovery team will need to talk with the child about her feelings, worries and anxieties. Equally, the family placement team will need to talk about the same subjects with the new family. It is sometimes tempting in this process to deny the less positive feelings about the move for fear that this would somehow prevent it from happening. However, the reverse is often the case: unspoken fears and anxieties denied will usually be acted out and presented in less manageable forms, which may then lead to a rejection by either party (Pughe and Philpot, 2007).

The team will be engaged in numerous practical tasks – the minutiae that provide the sure foundation for a successful move. These include:

- keeping records
- considering educational matters and financial considerations (like the settling-in grant and travel expenses)
- notifying the local-authority's medical adviser
- liaising with the foster family, and
- deciding dates when the child's progress will be considered.

The information about the child gathered through therapy, life-story work and therapeutic parenting should be shared with the new family as it will prove invaluable to them in understanding the child's strengths and weaknesses, her history, an analysis of her internal working model, and her likely reaction to events. This will assist the family in managing a child's behaviour within specific boundaries.

The child's residential home is where the process of the move begins and her future family should visit her there. The child's key carer is involved at the beginning, but after that the meetings will be between the child and the new family. At the same time, the child will be making visits of increasing length to the new family home. On these occasions there can be rehearsals for regular routines (like going to school) that will eventually take place from the new foster home. These visits to the new home also allow the child to transfer emotionally and physically. This is something that will initiate the grieving process but can also be used to diminish fears and worries for the future.

The key carer and the recovery team must give the child the reassurance she will need about the impending move and the new family. It is important, therefore, that they are able to observe positive interactions and communications between the two parties. The key carer has become someone whom the child can trust and rely upon and so she will look to him for positive and negative cues to confirm her own anxieties or excitement. The key carer's ability gradually to 'hand over' the child to the care and authority of the new family is one that is very important. One way in which this can symbolically take place is by the 'handing over' of the child's life-story book. This can demonstrate to the child that the key carer believes that the new family can welcome and look after the 'whole' of what she is, her past as well as her present and future. The new family then have the opportunity to confirm their ability and wish to do so (Pughe and Philpot 2007).

It is important, therefore, that in this transition period residential care continues to offer safety through its structures, and that there is the chance to clarify issues with trusted people to whom the child is attached, like the key carer. Throughout the transition period, too, it is important to review the progress made and the pace of activity. It may be necessary to slow things down and offer additional support and opportunities to reflect on the process. Regular review meetings allow continual review of what has been achieved, whether it has been done and what the results were. These meetings manage both details and the many feelings aroused by the move.

Pughe and Philpot (2007) state:

> Equally important is a recognition that the grieving process does not suddenly end when something new comes along. Careful attention needs to be paid to planning the child's continuing contact with significant members of the recovery team. Planning the calendar year ahead can highlight important events and dates for the child who would perhaps benefit from some sort of contact like birthdays, Christmas and anniversaries. Any of these may trigger intense feelings and a simple card or telephone call could help the child manage these reoccurring emotions. However, it is essential this kind of contact is planned beforehand and the child expects it, as unplanned individual acts of contact may be more about inability to let go rather than assist in letting go. (pp.129–130)

The last planning meeting should set the agenda for the future contacts for the child with the key carer and staff who are left behind by the child as she moves forward. Consideration should be given to the frequency, duration and location of these meetings, so that their purpose is clearly defined as supportive and not undermining. Taking responsibility for a child is not an easy task, and carers can become overwhelmed with the enormity of the task and the emotions involved. While the role of their fostering social worker is important in this regard, it should also be recognized that there is value in having a series of continuing professional support meetings that will involve key carers. These meetings allow the fostering team to use the understanding of the previous team, so that the care provided can be maintained and informed.

As the placement approaches, a final review meeting will be held to confirm the placement. Before this meeting, there will be a couple of days with no contact between the parent and child to allow for thought and reflection. At this period it is important that the carers and the child have the time to work through their feelings and worries about placement and are able to confirm and commit to the placement. Then comes the realization that the move is imminent, and there will be a saying of goodbyes and a celebration farewell party. Following the confirmation date, children often begin to reject the home staff because they are moving on. Often children want to dissociate themselves from the thought that they have ever lived in a children's home, because they are now 'normal' like everyone else, like their friends who live in families.

Questions

- Recall a time when you have started something new, perhaps a new job or a new relationship. What were your feelings about it, negative and positive?

- What preparation did you undertake for this? What preparation do you think others undertook?

- Reflecting on some of the themes presented in this book, imagine you are planning a placement for a child. What key events or elements would you build into the plan? List the range of emotions that might be present for the child, the new carers, new brothers and sisters, the current carers, and the other children with whom the child shares residential care.

- How could these emotions be thought about within your organization or care setting?

Another kind of fostering: the practice family

For children whose experience of families (within their own birth family or within foster care) is so negative, the intention must be that their understanding of families will change so that they regard them as safe and secure – because it is within a family that, at some point in the future, they will be living. This is not something that happens overnight, and nor does it happen because we say it should. Bringing children to a positive view of families, creating within them an internalization that families are a safe place in the world and in their lives, is a slow process.

For some children it is too big a move from the safety and security of residential care to go straight to being placed with a family. However, it is not always possible to determine whether a child or young person is actually able to live again in a family. In order to make this move, they may need to experience family life while still having the safety and security of the residential establishment behind them. This will allow them to explore issues and ideas, while not being asked to form life-long attachments: the experience is just one to enjoy. It is this that has given rise to the concept of the 'practice family'. This is an opportunity that requires careful matching in order for a child to spend one weekend a month and maybe two weeks in the summer holidays with a family.

For those families with knowledge of the history of fostering, being a practice family is not dissimilar to the old concept of the social uncle and aunt who would befriend a child in residential care. However, that idea has fallen out of fashion because it was rooted in the needs and wishes of adults rather than children. The concept of the practice family is based on the needs of children and what is best for them. It is the child who practises living in a family, not the family that practises caring for someone else's child. This very important difference in the tone and contact can be seen in the specific aims for the practice family which are that practice families should:

- offer an experience of family life in a family

- help children explore their feelings about families

- show children and young people the similarities with, and differences from, safe residential care

- help children to re-establish trust in families

- help children learn the realities of families – the boredom as well as the fun

- help children and young people understand that families are different to residential care homes; and

- help children understand that families will not necessarily entirely revolve around them.

The task of practice families is a highly specialized one and such families are a valuable part of the recovery team since they can offer other members information in the recovery and assessment process about the nature of the recovery and the child's inner working model. It is not an easy job and carers in such families need extensive training, with excellent placement support and supervision. Carers in this role need supervision about their own feelings and help in practising their responses to the child.

It is a complex task for families, but it does help children dispel myths about how families function. On occasions it can be summed up 'as doing ordinary, mundane things in a family, rather than have things done for you all the time'. Over time, a successful practice family placement helps children feel more confident about families in general and recognize in a small way that their internal working model has changed and that families can be safe and secure.

Carers who offer practice family placements receive the same assessment and training as carers who offer long-term placements. We believe practice families are a valuable resource that can have significant impact on the child, and therefore need to be matched appropriately, and have the same amount of time spent on planning and introductions as any full-time placement.

The use of practice families is based on clearly defined boundaries regarding:

- roles
- the length of time with the family (that is, no more than two weekends per month)
- tasks to complete (which are stated); and
- time limits as appropriate (no longer than 12 months).

The system is supported by

- therapeutic consultation for fostering social worker and carers as required
- regular foster home supervision; and

- an integrated support system, which includes a 24-hour on-call service. (This support system also offers access to training groups and support, access to support groups of carers and membership of the professional body Fostering Network.)

Over time, a successful practice family placement helps children feel more confident about families and recognize that their internal working model is changing. This is further progression in the process of recovery, and a step towards living permanently in a family. We anticipate that such change will take a minimum of six months, and possibly up to 12 months or more.

Clearly some questions arise in relation to a model that can encourage a child to form attachments, and then curtails them. However, practice family placements are not about making and breaking attachments. Rather, they are to enable children to realize and understand that families can be safe, and can offer good times. Often children enjoy practice family placement, and almost inevitably in the process someone will ask, often the social worker or key carer, if she can stay long term. Current thinking is that that this should not happen as the tasks of a practice family placement and long-term placement are very different and require different skills. If placements are allowed to drift into long-term placements, they have not been founded on trust and honesty, and this undermines the idea that family life is to be trusted.

Fostering literature and placement histories have stories about children coming for a short time and staying for longer. When these placements go wrong, there is often a great deal of recrimination, and it is clear that very powerful emotions take over and people frequently blame others (for example, children say carers are different now and carers say children are not grateful), while not taking any responsibility themselves. In thinking of long-term placements, we should always ask what the child's placement needs are, as well as asking why they have arisen and how the placement will help meet them.

If, in going through these considerations, a known family seems appropriate, then it might be possible to consider that family alongside others for the child. It is important that correct decisions, not easy decisions, are made, and that we avoid children feeling that they are pinballs who are being bounced into placements. Thus, it is the best possible long-term placement which should be sought, not that which is most convenient or easiest to find. A practice family placement is a stepping stone to a possible long-term placement, which can reassure children and the team around them, about their readiness for such a placement. It is not a short-cut way to preparation for that placement.

When a placement is made with a long-term carer, it does not necessarily mean the end of contact between the practice family and the child. In all instances, carers in practice families have a key role in supporting the child as she moves into a long-term placement, where that is considered appropriate. This may mean that they can have a role as the long-term family's respite carer for the child. But this is a consequent consideration, which may or may not emerge from the practice family placement. The essence of the placement is to meet the needs of a child in her moving toward an acceptance that a family is where she should be and that, ultimately, one will be selected that is best placed to meet her well-being.

The practice family and long introductions

There is always a danger, when considering the needs of children, of opting for the seemingly least detrimental alternative or the option that is most easily achievable. For example, short-term placements can go well and be confirmed as long-term placements, but at adolescence with the first hurdle of challenging behaviour and acting-out problems, breakdowns can occur. When this happens, the common factors are that there has been insufficient planning and a lack of training for the carer for the tasks involved. This can mean, therefore, that the placements do not meet the placement needs of either the child or the carer.

It is important, then, to distinguish between practice families and long introductions and to know how each, in their different ways, meet a child's needs. Thus, before we discuss the concept of practice families in detail, we will look at these differences:

Practice families allow a child to practise living in families, becoming safe with the idea that she *can* live in a family. They are not about children being seduced into a family and into making attachments, and neither are they a way of having backdoor long introductions. They must be presented to children as having very clear boundaries and expectations, which should be honoured and respected.

Introductions, on the other hand, are about helping the child move from one placement to the next placement (for example, from residential care to foster care, from the short-term to the long-term foster home) and are part of the process of forming long-term attachments. This can be a frightening proposition for traumatized children and much careful and considerate handling is required so that the various stages of shock, elation, withdrawal, and going forward can be worked out with the child's current carers, and can lead to the child acquiring a safe attachment. The need for long introductions is necessary because the integration of the child into her future family needs to be done at the correct pace and with caution because of their assessed need and proven history. Slipping from a practice family into a process of long introductions to the same family *can* happen but it should be guarded against because it does not allow the child to trust the intentions of the adults.

It is possible that a child has previous knowledge of potential carers because for example, they may be relatives or family friends. However, this does not obviate the need for the approach we describe here or the asking of the questions we have suggested need asking.

On occasion there may be a strong feeling that attachment bonds are being formed. When this happens, there needs to be very careful consideration of what to do next. Our suggestion would be that the normal process for matching should be followed while considering:

- what the child's needs are
- what are the skills and qualities required by the carers to meet those needs
- whether this family has those skills and qualifications; and
- how the family will use these skills and qualities to meet the child's placement needs.

Only in exceptional circumstances should practice family placements become long term. If the question arises, then the whole process of matching and introductions should begin again, as a clean sheet, so to speak, and the questions be raised about how and why this family meets the child's needs, as they would be for any long-term placement. When these questions can be answered openly and honestly then it should be possible to make a considered decision whether or not the placement should be long term. If there is agreement on this, the process of introductions can begin as if there has been no contact, so that the child can be claimed in the way we describe above when discussing introductions.

CHAPTER 6

How Placements Can Succeed

Throughout the UK, foster care has become the increasingly favoured way of caring for looked-after children. This fact and the diverse methods of fostering now available (from the short-term emergency placement to therapeutic and remand fostering) has nevertheless brought with it certain concerns. Fostering is not a cure-all and its use can, at times, be problematic (Berridge and Cleaver 1987; Farmer *et al.* 2004; Sinclair 2005).

With the *Quality Protects* and *Every Child Matters* initiatives government has recognized the importance of placement stability and the ways in which foster care can contribute to the well-being of children and young people. Local authorities are now required not to move children more than three times in a year, which has led to an encouraging decrease in the number of moves above this figure. Supporting and maintaining placements has, therefore, been seen as crucial in helping all children develop and achieve the outcomes set in *Every Child Matters*, which were:

- being healthy
- staying safe
- enjoying and achieving
- making a positive contribution; and
- achieving economic well-being (HM Treasury 2003).

One of these outcomes is of particular importance for traumatized children – staying safe. Their inner working model will tell them that carers and families are unsafe, insecure and unstable. The creation of a sense of stability for children, so that they come to trust others – importantly, families – will increase their sense of being safe. Helping traumatized children recover requires that their placements are stable, and that their entry or movement into the foster care system is not complicated by further multiple moves.

Critical to working with children and young people to this end is the support and supervision that agencies offer to placements, something on which many local authorities, voluntary bodies and independent fostering agencies place a high emphasis. The literature from agencies commonly mentions:

- regular supervision (weekly, fortnightly, monthly)
- initial and continuing training
- the provision of a named fostering social worker
- 24-hour support and supervision
- immediate response in time of need
- access to a range of consultants and therapists
- professional fees
- respite care
- the opportunity to obtain qualifications through NVQ or degree; and
- membership of Fostering Network or other professional organizations.

With so exhaustive a list, the question must be asked why placements ever fail, but the fact is that they do. This implies that there are other factors rather than provision of the service that can have a direct impact on the suitability of the placement. If this is the case, what needs considering are additional factors such as the placement history of the young person and also the histories of the carers, the integration and interaction of the services offered, and the framework within which they offered. Placement support should not begin as the placement comes into effect. It should begin before the process of matching and introductions when the child's placement needs are being identified and carers are being assessed.

Foster care cannot meet the placement needs of all the children all of the time, yet it is always the first resort for children in care and, thus, it is sometimes, used inappropriately. The frequency of placement failure (and the many moves which some children make as a result before entering residential care) is eloquent testimony to this, along with anecdotal evidence about carers being encouraged to take children for fostering when this is inappropriate due to the number of children the carers are already fostering and the conflicting needs of the children.

A careful matching of a child to a family and a good process of introduction provides the bedrock for a successful placement. For traumatized children (and, indeed all children) it is important that from the outset children recognize that this is different from the past – and that is what appropriate introductions do. The placement should be one that is planned and thought out, not one that is reactive and chosen at short notice. Good introductions establish this and confirm the challenge to the child's internal working model about families. Equally, it is important that the family placement team recognizes that the placement is different from previous placements, i.e. that it is the correct placement for the child with carers who have the right skills and qualities rather than just the fact of being able to offer the next or only available bed.

When this is done, support of different kinds can be used to ensure that the placement has the best chance of success, even if guarantees cannot be absolute. Key to this is how support services are offered – they need to be used together in a co-ordinated and integrated way with a clear purpose. However, care must be taken that the role of the carer is not lost in the over-provision of other professional help.

Let us take the example of nine-year-old Chloe who was placed with foster carers. The placement lasted for 18 months and had began well, but in the last nine months the carers had struggled with Chloe's increasingly challenging and destructive behaviour. This made them feel that they were not safe with her because of her violent outbursts when she would throw objects, cause damage, and hit them. In order to support the placement, the carers were provided with fortnightly visits, access to a support group and a therapeutic consultant, regular respite, and liaison with Chloe's school and school counsellor. Chloe was also allocated a therapist.

The carers asked for additional therapeutic support and help and for the child to have increased respite. The family-placement social worker discussed the case with his supervisor, who as a result of the carers having undergone family therapy, was able to see that more of the same could be offered. However, the supervisor doubted that the additional request for help would achieve anything in the placement. The family-placement social worker and his manager decided to offer caring for the carer, by making frequent visits, offering support and practical advice so that they felt cared for. This meant that there was increased frequency of visiting by the fostering social worker to the carers and to the school; a concentration on the carers' reactions to the child; an appropriate end to all the therapy, giving one person therapeutic oversight; and the co-ordination of regular meetings of the family placement team.

The result was that all the parties worked together, and that the carers were empowered to care for Chloe, and show her what they could do. The carers were able to help her make progress. The key to progress in this case was ensuring that the carers were made the healing agent of change (Kunstal 1998) and, feeling supported, that they had the responsibility for the child and the task.

Here, then, was a successful co-ordinated approach, which brought in an increasing amount of outside help. The wide array of support available did not disguise the fact that the carers have a therapeutic role, and they were helped to realize this. It is part of this role that carers should assist children to acknowledge the past and to recognize pain. Carers should not rush the process, and must work at accepting the child while rejecting her inappropriate behaviour. Such complex messages may, on occasion, be difficult for traumatized children to receive because, for example, their inner working model may be telling them that they are bad, and that if all this help is needed to manage them, then they cannot be managed.

A long-term placement should aim to continue the child's recovery by building on and consolidating the recovery work done in residential care. The carers and other members of the team should meet regularly to review the assessment and the recovery plan.

The recovery process during family placement involves an assessment and measurement process, which is effective and simple to use:

- providing a mechanism for identifying additional help needed

- providing a way of improving practice within family placement

- offering a forum for placement planning and to assist discussion at six-monthly reviews of the child's recovery and her needs; and

- ensuring the placement aims and outcomes are constantly reviewed and updated.

This is similar to recovery assessment in residential care as discussed by Tomlinson and Philpot (2008).

None of this is to provide a diagnostic tool, but rather to create a format for asking questions about each child, so that our understanding can develop and, as a result, our approach with each child be better informed. It will also help us ascertain areas of need for the child.

There are positive times and worrisome times in placement and external events can also have their impact on it, but the recovery programme offers a framework and a consistent method of looking at the placement. It provides the backdrop for assessing and understanding the behaviour. The starting point, however, is the carer herself, and her understanding of feelings. There is a need for her to move beyond the initial response and recognize in her own reactions to events what lies within her. The carer will also need to distinguish between what her feelings are for the child and what feelings the child has. Supervision and consultancy are important in helping both carers and family-placement social workers recognize and understand this process. It is important also for carers and social workers to recognize the potential impact on them of working with traumatized children – for example, the process of transference, projection and secondary traumatic stress disorder (Myers and Cornille 2002).[10]

Therapeutic parenting can help prevent the child from entering a negative attachment cycle because it recognizes that ordinary parenting is not enough when parenting traumatized children. The traumatized child whose internal working model does not recognize secure relationships within a family will not be able to connect or respond to ordinary parenting methods, which can then become punitive because of the lack of reaction given or progress made. Therapeutic parenting, in which carers are supervised by fostering social workers, is a key to successful placements. This way of working aims to see the child rather than her behaviour and the mask this creates.

It is important to understand the response that the child makes to her trauma. Often this will cause her to function emotionally at a lower age than her chronological age. Thus, we need to assess at what emotional age she is actually functioning and respond accordingly, and bridge the gap between emotional and chronological ages. This approach uses the extensive information available to assess the needs of the child, and to see how those needs are being met by the behaviour. The recovery model and the links to residential care, give access to information from colleagues in therapeutic parenting, therapy and life story, who can assist our understanding of the child, and the behaviour she is showing.

The recovery programme offers a hypothesis about what feelings cause the child to act as she does. It can also help us encourage her to acknowledge what we think about this and ask her to think about what might be influencing her in how she acts. In all of this, the positive feelings one has for the child must be remembered so that that the responsibility both for the behaviour and for managing it are placed in perspective.

When feelings are acknowledged and different methods are used to help express them, those feelings will be safer for the child to experience. Two ways to do this are by offering the child different choices, so that she can look at cause and effect, and also encouraging her to talk about the behaviour and its cause.

While, ultimately, behaviour has to be managed – and, in some cases, this will be immediately – the aim is to think about the experience and offer a different rationale for the behaviour in the current context. This is done by exploration, through linking previous experience to the current situation. The response in the past may have been appropriate – for example, it may have been about survival – but it needs to be different now. This is because environment and context have changed, and the child's internal working model has been changed by the safe environment and secure base and attachments offered, as well as the therapeutic recovery work which has been carried out with her.

This approach is seeking to offer a more healthy relationship between child and adult relationship in which the child's feelings are given recognition and validity. It is also where the child is praised and acknowledged for her positive interactions which promote her sense of self-esteem and self-worth. This is to create integration and congruence between the child's thoughts, feelings and actions in the present. It allows the child to trust her carer and to recognize that they can keep her safe and that she will be allowed to grow and change. From this the child can develop a sense of trust and attachment. The relationship between child and parent can thus move from one of confrontation, where the relationship is based on a negative attachment cycle, to a positive attachment cycle, where carers can have fun and enjoy the relationship (Pughe and Philpot 2007).

Through using both themselves and their environment, the carers can enable a child to continue the process of integrating her thoughts, feelings and actions, and to build a better future for herself, so that she can trust and have fun and enjoy relationships. As Pughe and Philpot (2007) put it:

> Therapeutic parenting is about the change for each child to develop a primary attachment with one person, their key carer, which itself helps the child to develop her sense of self and her growing understanding of the needs of others and how she impacts upon them. (p.44)

The foster carer in this role provides nurturing care and allows the child to discuss her many emotions, while acting as the container for her complex emotions. In this way carers become active listeners (Archer 1999) and the child develops a sense of trust and attachment. The end of this process, if there ever is an end, is the development of a positive sense of self and an integrated identity based on a new set of relationships and an integration of the child's past experiences and present life.

A key component to the successful adaptation of an approach based on therapeutic parenting and what Archer (1999) calls active listening is the quality of supervision offered. Many agencies talk about offering supervision to their carers but this often seems based on the dictum that amateurs get support, professionals get supervision. However, all carers are professionals and should have supervision. In practice, many supervision sessions are no more than occasions where key outcomes are recorded and reported. Here supervision is a method of monitoring of effectiveness and reporting and does not look at the feelings generated.

It is important to recognize that this work produces powerful feelings and emotions. As we work with children who have been traumatized, our own traumas and losses can be triggered, however the children need us to separate our experiences from their own, so that we can stay attuned to *their* experiences and help *them*. This reflects the work of Cairns (2002) and

Schofield and Beek (2006a) and their training programme (Schofield and Beek 2006b).

In relation to the supervision of carers, the work needs to be guided in the manner explained by Tomlinson (2004), who refers to five aspects of what he calls 'the supervision of therapeutic work':

- Ensuring that each team member is aware of therapeutic matters and understands the basic approach.

- Creating the occasion when the concerns of the person supervised can be aired and explored.

- Training which allows the supervisor to help the supervisee to underpin his practice with theory.

- Managing in the sense of giving direction where necessary.

- Providing a reliable and protected space for supervision. (pp.176–177)

In order for carers to be offered supervision of this nature, their fostering social worker needs to recognize that their task is to move beyond the requirements set out in the *Fostering Services Regulations* (Department of Health 2002b), and to offer something that is more akin to oversight and the exploration of feelings. (Here one might question the role of unannounced visits as part of supervision, which tends to be more associated with child protection than the monitoring and reporting aspects of supervision.) By helping carers explore their own feelings, so that they are not damaging to the child's development, carers can develop what Archer (1999) describes as:

> an active listening approach to parents themselves. By acknowledging just how hard it can be to live alongside, and struggle to get close to, a child who hurts, we enable parents to acknowledge that they are not the problem – nor is the child or his behaviour. Instead, we reassure adoptive and foster parents that they are part of the solution for the child and seek to reframe the child's behaviour as attempts to reach resolution for himself.

In the example of Michael, aged 14, we can see how supervision can help. He had been placed for two years. In his first year, he made very good progress but didn't do so in his second year. As the placement was coming to the end of its second year, the school reported that he took a gun to school. This was a toy potato gun and had been taken from him by his carer until the school holidays. The school was upset by the incident and sought to exclude him, while the carers felt the school had over-reacted. The carers were also upset by the fact that Michael had taken the gun from their bedroom. Their very strong feelings about this were a surprise, but one of the workers, remembering the history of the carers – the woman had herself been abused – was able to talk to the carer about her comments about feeling violated in the past. It was important to deal with the carer's feelings that were not about the event, but the memories triggered in her. The carer knew that she could not stop Michael going into the bedroom (short of locking the door), but just needed to know whether or not he had been in the room. In which case, she would put a piece of paper in the door, which dropped when opened, but which she and her husband replaced if they went in.

Another key aspect of placement support is that of the therapeutic contribution to the placement. Traumatized children entering the care system bring with them numerous experiences, including those of physical, sexual and emotional abuse, neglect, abandonment, attachment problems, bereavement, and many others. Placements should begin from a presumption that therapeutic insight will be provided, and that a range of therapeutic options is open to the family placement team working with the child.

While there will be a break in therapy at the start of the foster placement in order to enable the child to concentrate on making a satisfactory move, it is intended that direct therapy with the child if needed will begin again after three to six months. The use of a different therapist during foster care may be appropriate, although this should be decided on the basis of the needs of each child. However, approaches to the child are made consistent through ensuring that the results of all direct therapy are fed back to carers and other professionals.

The empowering of carers can ensure that they can become the therapeutic resource for the child. This often means that the therapist works through the carers. Such work needs to complement the therapy offered to the child. Good communication is critical in maintaining links. The therapist must have a good awareness of what is happening in the child's daily life, for example, her relationships with carers and other children.

The work is done at the child's own pace, in a child-centred, to some extent non-directive manner. (It cannot be purely non-directive because the therapist may need to draw out particular issues from sessions or bring in issues from the child's life based on the therapist's assessment of the child's development.) It facilitates communication, verbal, non-verbal and symbolic, through play and the expressive arts (Rymaszewska and Philpot 2006).

Alongside the provision of therapeutic support, carers and the family placement team need to continue to progress the child's understanding of her own life. Children's histories should be shared freely with the carer, with the child present during the introductory process. An integral part of the placement process will be updating and reshaping the child's life-story book. Her story has not ended because she has moved, and we do not know everything that has happened to her. In placement there may be new triggers, which offer new information that the child will need to process and resolve.

Life-story work will be familiar to the child from her time in residential care and will be completed regularly and for special occasions. The information contained in the book will be seen during each monthly supervision visit by the family placement worker, and every two months (or, more frequently, if necessary) additional sheets will be added to the child's life-story book. Such work is another way (and an enjoyable one) in which the carers can show their continuing commitment to the child.

An example of how life-story work can arise from day-to-day incidents comes with the example of Peter, who was 13 and had been placed for three years. He approached his carer in the kitchen and was about to ask something. Because the carer was carrying hot fat, she asked Peter to move to another part of the kitchen for his safety. The request was made strongly, loudly and forcibly and Peter moved to a darker part of the kitchen. He was immediately reminded of his childhood experiences of loud voices and darkness, of being locked up in a cupboard. Peter swore at the carer and ran off. When he returned the carer talked to him about what had happened and how it linked, in his mind, to his past. Peter was then able to talk about his experiences of home, and a further chapter was able to be added to his life-story book.

As children grow up, so their understanding and knowledge expands and they can come to an increased understanding of their past and their future possibilities through a different perception of the events and people who have hitherto shaped their lives.

Caring safely

Fostering, as with so much work with children, carries with it an inherent risk. All work based on the idea of a relationship involves risk but perhaps the risk for foster carers is all the greater for the fact that, unlike other work with children, it is carried out in the private and intimate circumstances of the carer's own home. Thus, it is important to look at how to care safely. Too often training and advice given in this area talk of eliminating of risk, rather than discussing the management of acceptable risk. In the dealings of one human being with another risk can never be eliminated, no matter how tight the procedures, how strong the rules, or how good the supervision and monitoring. And even were it possible for risk to be eliminated, this would only produce emotionally sterile and functional environments for children, where they could never grow or learn about the power of suitable, intimate relationships.

Caring safely is about recognizing that having brought a traumatized child home with her, the foster carer has imported very powerful emotions into the family. Fostering will have an effect on all the family and can lead to an attack on fundamental ideas and beliefs that were previously regarded as jointly held by a couple and within a family. Traumatized children have the capacity to split and separate, so that a couple who foster end up disagreeing with each other, and strong relationships can be threatened. Foster families need to be aware of this and to talk openly between themselves and with their social worker about these issues and the threats that they feel under.

Every parent knows that a child's development includes risks that the parent has to assess as being acceptable or otherwise. Furthermore, as a child grows older – even the toddler as much as the baby, as well as the progression through the years – this is not just about parents saying that a risk can be taken or not. It is about helping the child to understand risk and how to meet it, so that, eventually, children become responsible, by varying degrees, for the decisions that they take. This is equally true for the foster carer but much more so because of the history of the child and the nature of the relationship between the child and the carer – and, indeed, the carer's immediate and wider family and those whom she welcomes into her home.

In making informed and appropriate choices carers require various things:

- First, they need full information about the child, in part through the sharing of all the information held through the life-story work, therapy and residential care that has been undertaken with the child.

- Carers also need appropriate training and preparation courses and high levels of support (also see Chapter 3).

- They also need written records and reports that note the child's progress and the rationale for the decisions taken.

This means working with a clearly defined safe caring agreement. This will entail that care is agreed by all the parties involved in the placement and then written down. The agreement needs to be an active document and not one that gathers dust on the shelf, only to be referred to in reviews. At each placement visit the agreement should be looked at and, when necessary, updated. It should also show the progress the child has made. Just as the original agreement is known to all, so should any changes to it that are made.

It is easy to drift into a way of caring that does not reflect the safe caring agreement. Often this can be a sign of progress, in which case it is important to note all changes, so that the agreement continues to reflect reality. For example, if a child now sits in the front of the car, this should be noted, rather than it just happening. Should allegations over this arise in the future, but the safe caring agreement says that riding in the front of the car does not happen because that was the practice when it was first drawn up, then neither carer nor child are safe.

Carers, therapists and other professionals

Carers and therapists cannot do it all themselves and there will always be a need for additional help and support. In the main this will come from the recovery, therapeutic and life-story staff, but other professional services, like psychiatrists, should also be available. Children and young people's behaviour can be discussed among such a group and seen in context. Psychologists can be used for team consultancy in relation to individual cases and the dynamics arising between the child and carers, carers and agency, agency and social workers, and workers within the team.

The opportunity for carers to meet with staff who have known the child and experienced the same feelings about them can be important for them. It can help them recognize that they are not doing wrong and that the child is going through a process of testing out. It is also helpful for the child to know that there is continuity and that in relation to safety and containment, those who have cared for her previously are still involved.

It may be appropriate that contact with staff still employed by the agency, who were previously involved with the child, be maintained. These may include the key carer, staff and manager from the residential home where the child was placed.

The three and a half years of the recovery programme should be seen as providing a solid foundation from which the young people can move forward as they go into the less structured environment of family life and in to society. It should be expected that when children and young people move, there is joy and excitement, followed by worry, anxiety and concern. The model we are postulating, therefore, can have sharp recovery over the initial period in residential care, followed by a dip in the transition stage, and a steady recovery over a longer period in foster care. No child's life (like that of anyone else) can be adequately seen as linear because throughout it is likely to be punctuated by peaks and troughs, and the exact timing of the dip will be related to individual circumstances and events. The literature on foster care means that foster carers and fostering social workers will be familiar with the idea of a honeymoon period at the start of placements, followed by a period of challenging behaviour and this would be similar to the dip mentioned previously. We might question if appropriate introductions affect the idea of a honeymoon period with the dip managed by the residential staff and appropriate time taken over introductions.

In foster care, Tomlinson and Philpot's (2008) 24 outcomes for recovery are the solid base. The child's response to these individual outcomes is then developed in a variety of settings like home, school, with foster family, with the birth family through contact with them, with friends and other children, at clubs, and on holiday.

We need to explore the following questions: How is the child able to respond in each of these individual situations to the individual recovery outcomes? How successful is she in meeting her individual recovery outcomes and for what amount of the time? The consistency of the relationships in various settings will assist achievement of the individual recovery outcomes and offer an indication of change and a changing inner working model.

What sustains placements is:

- the correct assessment of children's readiness for fostering

- the professional training of carers

- planned introductions based on attachment theory

- placement, supervision, support and consultancy; and

- the use of the recovery programme to inform understanding and practice.

Questions

- Think of how you viewed a particular event during your childhood and then how you viewed it as an adult. What are the differences and what causes these differences?

- Did this recollection give you a sense of *déjà vu*? What prompted this?

- Have you experienced occasions where events have reminded you of another event and when does this happen?

CHAPTER 7

Toward Independence

Gaining independence is one of the greatest markers in the first 25 years of life. It is not so much an event – whereby one is one person one day and another the next – so much as a process, a period of experiences (social, psychology and familial) that accumulate in a realization that a certain time has been reached when one will step into the wider world. It is a time of transition, moving from one stage of life, when one's decisions and room for manoeuvre are, at very least, influenced by, and sometimes directed by, others to a stage when one gains autonomy. The chance to make decisions (and mistakes) and to accept responsibilities is much greater than even the many legal responsibilities placed on the young person at this time.

Independence is a time of looking forward, turning one's back on adolescence and childhood, a time when school examinations indicate future possibilities, and when the family home seems less attractive than a home of one's own. It is also a time when from being, for example, the oldest in the family or a member of the senior year at school, you are, so to speak, starting again: one becomes the newest member of staff in the company or a fresher at university. For young people making this transition, this is a process of becoming interdependent rather than totally dependent.

All of this is not easily understood by young people; there seems to be almost too much to accommodate to despite all the apparent attractions of being 'an adult'. For most young people raised in their own families, parents strike a balance between enabling the young person to move forward to this new stage of life, while always being there to offer support – a bed for the night when needed, financial support at university, money to make up for the shortcomings of wages in the first job, and, of course, support and advice. Most parents do not regard 16, 18 or even 21 as an age when their children have to fend for themselves, materially or emotionally. They may think that it is a time when their children will have to learn from their own mistakes but not without them keeping a watchful eye on their offspring.

Yet this is not the case for many young people leaving care. The gradualness of transition for their peers is replaced by the arbitrariness of what will happen to them when they reach 18, either through a move or a change of status to Supported Lodgings. Many local authorities automatically cut off foster placements at 18. One young woman was told, when in the middle of her A-level course at further education college when just 17, that she would have to find her own accommodation (Ajayi and Quigley 2006). Such actions, the same authors find, are 'sadly common'. For foster carers, in such situations, the problem is that they wish to continue to care for the young person but cannot afford the loss of income when their allowances stop.

Most young people achieve independence, with their families' help, when they are of an age that they want it and are ready for it. A functional age can be below the emotional age. However, again this is not so for looked-after young people. The age of 18 rests on a blanket but mistaken assumption that all young people; including those who are looked after, reach both emotional and social maturity and are functionally and emotionally adept in a way that readies them for 'independence'.

Thus, young people who have been in care will have many of the same expectations and fears about advancing toward independence as their conttemporaries but they will often do so without any of the parental support that so many contemporaries enjoy. Parental responsibility of the local authority ceases on the young person's 18th birthday. Some young people will have been in the care of foster carers who regard them as family and are not willing to let them go off on their own just because they are 18. Many, many carers do this but they do so through their own concern, compassion and goodwill. Local authorities will not make payment or offer the support to allow them to continue formally to foster. However, there can be ways around this. Some local authorities make financial arrangements to allow foster carers to offer Supported Lodgings for the young person thus allowing fostering to continue *de facto* until the young person is 21.

In a decade which has seen several pieces of legislation and policy statements aimed at improving the situation of children and young people generally, the Children (Leaving Care) Act 2000 represented a recognition of much that was wrong with existing services. This was a shift to put care leavers at the centre of attention, and create a radical new direction for services. The Act reasserted 18 as the age for leaving care when, by default, it had very often settled at 16. It encouraged witholding discharge from care until the young person was prepared and ready. It extended the duty of local authorities to care for and support young people leaving care in the transition years until they reached 21 for those who could not return to their families. Local authorities were also obliged to offer financial support and accommodation to those in full-time education until the age of 24.

Although there are no comparable figures about the respective living arrangements for those leaving care and young people generally, it is generally considered that 24 is the average when most young people leave home. Simon and Owen (2006), quoting figures from the former Department for Education and Skills in 2003, show that, on their 19th birthday:

- 11 per cent of care leavers were living with parents or relatives
- 15 per cent were in supported accommodation
- 4 per cent were in a community home
- 37 per cent were living independently
- 2 per cent were in custody
- 6 per cent in lodgings
- 6 per cent were classified as other (which included bed and breakfast and emergency accommodation)
- 19 per cent, however, were no longer in touch with their local authority and so where they were living was not known.

Too often 'independence' for young people leaving care is a false promise – advocated as a chance to be in charge of your own life and have your own home, little mention is made of the obverse side: being lonely and poor and on one's own. The Children and Young Person's Act, which made its way onto the statute book at the time of writing, should make sure that young people are not forced out of care before they are ready, by giving them a greater say over moves to independent living and ensuring that they retain support and guidance for as long as they need it.

However, local authorities maintaining responsibility for young people until they reach 21 is not without its questions. Young people of that age may well not welcome the oversight of a local authority – the visits and monitoring of social workers. One of the rights of independence and adulthood is not to have others, even well intentionally, poking their noses into your life. So any continuing relationship with statutory authorities needs to recognize that; it will have to be different in kind to what has gone before: much more of a light touch, at very least. There will be the tension of wanting to be seen to be a good parent but allowing the freedom that a good parent would allow. This is not easy for a local authority exercising statutory responsibilities and with responsibility for spending.

As it is, a young person who moves straight from a foster home to some kind of independent living is often placed in a self-contained flat or supported lodgings. Not only does she do this at an earlier age than con- temporaries living with their birth families but she is rarely supported in the same way as they are. Her foster family is no longer there (unless they choose to continue an 'unofficial' relationship) because the local authority is no longer paying them to look after her. 'Independence', in such circum- stances, may often mean confusion, bewilderment and a sense of abandonment. Even Supported Living, which has become a very popular way of accommodating young people leaving care, often implies help only when you really need it. In the main, other young people do get help from their parents when they need it but their parents also make sure that they feel able to ask for it – as do many foster carers.

After 18, while social workers can do much to help a young person, their role is not suited to offering the kind of 'parental' help that the foster carer had been able to offer before then. They cannot easily offer the day-to-day, intimate, informal interactions that help young people move on in life. That is why foster carers are best placed to continue to help care leavers.

The role of a foster carer once a young person leaves home is not as intense as hitherto but it is still about wanting to see the young person make progress. But this time it is progress in the wider world. The young person now needs the support and advice that others of their age and situation receive. But at this time, all young people are gaining a first taste of freedom and it is important that the foster carer – like the parent – combines help and advice with a respect for this growing autonomy and the young person's ability to make her own mistakes in achieving it, while also helping her to learn from them. There are, too, it should be remembered, thresholds to the mistakes that can be made. No responsible parent allows his child to make a mistake that is injurious to her. So the foster carer's help also involves teaching young people how to learn and how to develop the negotiating skills that underpin an independent life. A young person who feels that 'no one listens to me' may be saying that she has no one to rely on. Such fostering requires applying the understanding about therapeutic parenting without, at this age, the intensity of earlier years.

There is much, too, in this teaching, advice and support that is practical. One of the first things that anyone learns who sets up on their own is that day-to-day tasks and skills, like, say, cooking and managing money (which they may not have had to concern themselves with before), are the most pressing. These need to be taught.

The key to all of this is responsible and therapeutic parenting as compared with what can be seen as a *laissez-faire* attitude. It is the difference between saying 'Be in by 1 a.m.' and 'I'll come and collect you at 12.30'. It is about helping a young person to have a safe passage on the way to adulthood and her being conscious that that help is underlaid by concern and a readiness to help, and not interference.

Young people leaving care are like their contemporaries in that what is helpful to them in that transition from 18 to adulthood is a continuation of the advice and emotional and practical support that good parenting entails and that foster carers can give. Yet they are not like other young people in that the law and too much local-authority practice assumes that 18 represents a door through which they walk unaided. For those who have suffered abuse and been traumatized, such an arbitrary age begs a question too often overlooked: 'Why do we assume that recovery happens at 18 years of age?' Is it not more likely that the effect of treatment will be seen at, say, 28 when the young person will probably have settled into a relationship and her own children are not in care? If we viewed the development of young people in care as a gradual process – an idea that has underpinned so much of what we have said in this book – then we would adjust our placement policies to reflect the reality of their lives.

Notes

1 Private fostering, as defined by the Children Act 1989, is when a child under the age of 16 (18 if disabled) is placed for more than 28 days other than with a close relative, (defined as brother, sister, grandparent, aunt, or uncle) – *see* Philpot (2001). Private fostering, as its name suggests, is a private arrangement between parent and carer and is not considered in this book.

2 The terminology used in the past is instructive. Children were 'boarded out' and there was 'baby farming' which (for all the sometimes good intentions of those who thought they were seeking children's welfare) also has connotations of the care of animals.

3 The principle of working with parents rather than compulsorily through the courts.

4 A carer looking after a child who is placed following the granting of a residence order.

5 For a concise explanation of how the brain develops, works and the impact that abuse and trauma can have on it *see* Pughe and Philpot (2007). For a summary of research *see* Glaser (2001) and Balbernie (2001).

6 Dysregulation of affect is when emotions seem out of control: the person feels that they are about to burst with emotion and overwhelm themselves and others with it if allowed to do so. For children, this can show itself in play by fantasy, movement and speaking almost in voices, together with uncontrolled emotional outbursts unrelated to the play. Dysregulation of affect can show in children being defiant, anxious, unco-operative, depressed, impulse-ridden, oppositional, and acting unpredictably (James 1994).

7 *See* also Bowlby (1969, 1973–1980), Howe (1995) and Howe *et al.* (1999).

8 The Stockholm Syndrome derives from a bank robbery in Stockholm, Sweden, in August 1973. Four bank employees (three women and a man) were taken hostage by the bank robber, who took them with him into the vault and kept them there for 131 hours. When finally the hostages were freed, they seemed to have formed an emotional bond with their captor. The told reporters that they saw the police, rather than the robber as their enemy, and that they had positive feelings towards him.

9 Multi-dimensional foster care is a cost-effective alternative to residential treatment for adolescents with complex needs and challenging behaviour.

10 Secondary traumatic stress disorder is the process whereby people who are caring for, or involved with, someone who suffers trauma, also experience trauma themselves.

References

Adopted Child (1994) 'Variety of attachment disorders need variety of treatment options.' *13*, 5, May.

Ajayi, S. and Quigley, M. (2006) 'By Degrees: Care Leavers in Higher Education.' In E. Chase, A. Simon and S. Jackson (eds) *In Care and After. A Positive Perspective.* Abingdon: Routledge.

Aldgate, J. (1989) 'Foster families and residential care for older children: some interpersonal dynamics.' *Children and Society 3* (Spring), pp.19–36.

Ames, J. (1993) *We Have Learned a Lot from Them: Foster Care for Young People with Learning Difficulties.* Barkingside: National Children's Bureau/Barnardo's.

Archer, C. (1999) 'Reparenting the traumatised child: a developmental process.' *YoungMinds Magazine,* September/October.

Archer, C. (2003) 'Weft and Warp: Developmental Impact of Trauma and Implications for Healing.' In C. Archer and A. Burnell (eds) *Trauma, Attachment and Family Permanence: Fear Can Stop You Loving.* London: Jessica Kingsley Publishers.

Archer, C. and Burnell, A. (eds) (2003) *Trauma, Attachment and Family Permanence. Fear Can Stop You Loving.* London: Jessica Kingsley Publishers.

BAAF Adoption and Fostering (2008), '*Statistics*'. Available at www.baaf.org.uk

Balbernie, R. (2001) 'Circuits and circumstances: the neurobiological consequences of early relationship experiences and how they shape later behaviour.' *Journal of Child Psychotherapy 27*, 3, pp.237–255.

Barry, M. (2001) *A Sense of Purpose. Care Leavers' Views and Experiences of Growing Up.* Edinburgh: Save the Children.

Barth, R., Courtney, M., Berrick, J. and Albert, V. (1994) *From Child Abuse to Permanency Planning.* New York, NY: Aldine de Gruyter.

Bebbington, A. and Miles, J. (1990) 'The supply of foster families for children in care.' *British Journal of Social Work 20*, 4, pp.283–307.

Berridge, D. (1985) *Children's Homes.* Oxford: Blackwell.

Berridge, D. (2005) 'Fostering now: messages from research.' *Adoption and Fostering 29*, 4, Winter.

Berridge, D. and Cleaver, H. (1987) *Foster Home Breakdown.* Oxford: Basil Blackwell.

Borland, M., O'Hara, G. and Triseliotis, J. (1991) 'Placement outcomes for children with special needs.' *Adoption and Fostering 75*, 2, pp.18–28.

Boswell, J. (1991) *The Kindness of Strangers. The Abandonment of Children in Western Europe from Late Antiquity to the Renaissance.* Harmondsworth: Penguin Books.

Bowlby, J. (1969) *Attachment.* London: Hogarth Press.

Bowlby, J. (1973–1980), *Attachment Trilogy. Volumes I–III. London: Hogarth Press.*

Broad, B. (ed.) (2001) *Kinship Care: The Placement Choice for Children and Young People.* Lyme Regis: Russell House Publishing.

Broad, B., Hayes, R. and Rushforth, C. (2001) *Kith and Kin: Kinship Care for Vulnerable Young People.* York: Joseph Rowntree Foundation/London: National Children's Bureau.

Bullock, R. (2008) communication with one of the authors (Philpot).

Burnell, A. and Archer, C. (2003) 'Setting up the Loom: Attachment Theory Revisited.' In C. Archer and A. Burnell (eds) *Trauma, Attachment and Family Permanence: Fear Can Stop You Loving.* London: Jessica Kingsley Publishers.

Buscaglia, L. (1982) *Living, Loving and Learning.* Thorofare, NJ: Slack Books.

Cairns, K. (2002) *Attachment, Trauma and Resilience: Therapeutic Caring for Children.* London: BAAF Adoption and Fostering.

Chamberlain, P. (2003) *Treating Chronic Juvenile Offenders: Advances Made Through the Oregon Multidimensional Treatment Foster Care Model.* Washington, DC: American Psychological Association.

Committee on Local Authority and Allied Social Services (Seebohm Committee) (1968) *Report of the Committee on Local Authority and Allied Personal Social Services.* London: HMSO.

Connor, T., Sclare, I., Dunbar, D. and Elliffe, J. (1985) 'Making a life story book.' *Adoption and Fostering 9,* 2.

Curtis Committee (1946) *Report of the Care of Children Committee.* London: HMSO.

Department for Children, Schools and Families (2008) *Children Looked After in England (including Adoption and Care Leavers) Year Ending 31 March 2007.* National Statistics, 20 September 2007. London: Department for Children, Schools and Families.

Department for Education and Skills (2006) *Care Matters. Transforming the Lives of Children and Young People in Care.* London: The Stationery Office.

Department of Health (2002a) *Fostering for the Future.* London: The Stationery Office.

Department of Health (2002b) *Fostering Services Regulations.* London: The Stationery Office.

Department of Health, Social Services and Public Safety (2008) *Children Order Statistical Bulletin.* Belfast: Community Information Branch.

Fahlberg, V. (2003) *A Child's Journey Through Placement.* London: BAAF Adoption and Fostering.

Farmer, E., Moyers, S. and Lipscombe, J. (2004) *Fostering Adolescents.* London: Jessica Kingsley Publishers.

Fein, E., Maluccio, A. N., Hamilton, V. J. and Ward, D. E. (1983) 'After foster care: permanency planning for children.' *Child Welfare 62,* 6.

Fostering Network (2007) *Scottish Executive's National Fostering and Kinship Care Strategy: Consultation: February 2007: Consultation with Young People.* London: Fostering Network.

Gibson, F. (2004) *The Past in the Present. Reminiscence Work in Health and Social Care.* Baltimore, MD: Health Professions Press.

Glaser, D. (2001) 'Child abuse, neglect and the brain: a review.' *Journal of Child Psychology and Psychiatry and Allied Disciplines 41,* 1, pp.97–116.

Gray, G. (2002) 'Best Laid Plans: Concurrent Planning.' In A. Douglas and T. Philpot (eds) *Adoption: Changing Families, Changing Times.* London: Routledge.

Gray, P. and Parr, E. (1957) *Children in Care and the Recruitment of Foster Parents.* London: Home Office.

Greeff, R. (ed.) (1999) *Fostering Kinship: An International Perspective on Foster Care by Relatives.* Aldershot: Avebury.

Guishard-Pine, J., McCall, S. and Hamilton, L. (2007) *Understanding Looked After Children. Psychology for Foster Care.* London: Jessica Kingsley Publishers.

Haight, B. (1998) 'Use of Life Review/Life Story Books in Families with Alzheimer's Disease.' In P. Schweitzer (ed.) *Reminiscence in Dementia Care.* London: Age Exchange.

Hazel, N. (1981) *A Bridge to Independence.* Oxford: Blackwell.

HM Treasury (2003) *Every Child Matters.* London: The Stationery Office.

Holman, B. (1995) *The Evacuation. A Very British Revolution.* Oxford: Lion Publishing.

Holman, B. (2002) Letter, *Community Care,* 27 August–4 September.

Holman, R. (1973) *Trading in Children: A Study in Private Fostering.* London: Routledge & Kegan Paul.

Home Office (1965) *The Child, The Family and the Young Offender.* London: HMSO.

Home Office (1968) *Children in Trouble.* London: HMSO.

House of Commons Social Services Committee (1984) (Short Report) *Children in Care 1.* London: HMSO.

Howe, D. (1995) *Attachment Theory for Social Work Practice.* Basingstoke: Macmillan.

Howe, D. (2000) 'Attachment.' In M. Davies (ed.) *The Blackwell Encyclopaedia of Social Work.* Oxford: Blackwell.

Howe, D., Brandon, M., Hinings, D. and Schofield, G. (1999) *Attachment Theory, Child Maltreatment and Family Support.* Basingstoke: Macmillan.

Hudson, J. and Galloway, B. (1989) *Specialist Foster Care: A Normalizing Experience.* New York, NY: Haworth Press.

Hunt, J., Waterhouse, S. and Lutman, E. (2008) *Keeping Them in the Family. Outcomes for Children Placed in Kinship Care through Care Proceedings.* London: BAAF Adoption and Fostering.

Hunter, M. (2001) *Psychotherapy and Young People in Care: Lost and Found.* Hove: Brunner-Routledge.

James, B. (1994) *Handbook for Treatment of Attachment-Trauma Problems in Children.* New York, NY: The Free Press.

Kahan, B. (1979) *Growing Up in Care.* Oxford: Blackwell.

Kane, S. (2007) *Care Planning for Children in Residential Care.* London: National Children's Bureau.

Kelly, G. and Gilligan, R. (eds) (2000) *Issues in Foster Care.* London: Jessica Kingsley Publishers.

Kirton, D., Beecham, J. and Ogilvie, K. (2007) 'Still the poor relations? Perspectives on valuing and listening to foster carers.' *Adoption & Fostering 31,* 3, pp.6–17, Autumn.

Kosensen, M. (1993) 'Descriptive study of foster and adoptive care services in a Scottish agency.' *Community Alternative 5,* 2, Fall.

Kübler-Ross, E. (1970) *On Death and Dying.* London: Tavistock.

Kunstal, F. (1998) 'Mending fractured lives: understanding and strategies for helping troubled children.' Workshop handouts. May.

Lahti, J. (1982) 'A follow-up study of foster children in permanent placements.' *Social Services Review.* Chicago, IL: University of Chicago.

Longford Committee (1964) *Crime: A Challenge to Us All.* London: Labour Party.

Maginn, C. (2006) 'Pillar talk.' *Community Care.* 16–22 March.

Marsh, P. and Peel, M. (1999) *Leaving Care in Partnership: Family Involvement with the Children Act 1969.* London: The Stationery Office.

Maslow, A. H. (1954) *Motivation and Personality.* New York, NY: Harper and Row.

McAndrew, G. (2000) 'Fostering or adoption: doubts, dilemmas and decision making – the impact on children.' Paper given to conference, Tavistock Clinic, London, August.

McGill, P. (2003) 'Kinship Care: A Child in the Family.' In A. Douglas and T. Philpot (eds) *Adoption: Changing Families, Changing Times,* London: Routledge.

Miens, E. (1997) *Security of Attachment and the Social Development of Cognition.* Hove: Psychology Press.

Morgan, P. (1998) *Adoption and the Care of Children: The British and American Experience.* London: Institute for Economic Affairs.

Mumford, A. (ed) (1998) *Gower Handbook of Management Development.* Aldershot: Gower. 4th edition.

Myers, T.W. and Cornille, T.A. (2002) 'The Trauma of Working with Traumatised Children.' In C. Figley (ed.) *Treating Compassion Fatigue.* Hove: Brunner-Routledge.

National Foster Care Association (1998) *Policy Statement: Family and Friends as Foster Carers.* London: National Foster Care Association.

National Implementation Team (2007) *Multidisciplinary Treatment Foster Care in England (MDTFC).* 3rd Annual Progress Report. London: Department for Children, Schools and Families, July.

Parker, R. (1990) *Away from Home. A Short History of Provision for Separated Children.* Barkingside: Barnardo's.

Perry, B. and Szalavitz, M. (2006) *The Boy Who Was Raised as a Dog.* New York, NY: Basic Books.

Philpot, T. (1994) *Action for Children. The Story of UK's Foremost Children's Charity.* Oxford: Lion Publishing.

Philpot, T. (2001) *A Very Private Practice. An Investigation into Private Fostering.* London: BAAF Adoption and Fostering.

Philpot, T. (2003) Interview conducted by one of the authors. Unpublished MS. (Unless otherwise attributed, quotations from children come from the same source.)

Pointon, C. (2004) 'The future of trauma work,' CPJ online. www.bacp.co.uk/cpj/current/trauma.htm, accessed 12 November 2008.

Pugh, G. (2007) *London's Forgotten Children. Thomas Coram and the Foundling Hospital.* Stroud, Glos: Tempus Publishing.

Pughe, B. and Philpot, T. (2007) *Living Alongside a Child's Recovery. Therapeutic Parenting with Traumatized Children.* London and Philadelphia: Jessica Kingsley Publishers.

Richards, A. (2001) *Second Time Around: A Survey of Grandparents Raising Their Grandchildren.* London: Family Rights Group.

Rose, R. and Philpot, T. (2005) *The Child's Own Story. Life Story Work with Traumatized Children.* London: Jessica Kingsley Publishers.

Rowe, J. and Lambert, L. (1973) *Children who Wait.* London: Association of Agencies for Adoption and Fostering.

Rowe, J., Hundleby, M. and Keane, A. (1984) *Long-term Foster Care.* London: Batsford.

Ruegger, M. and Rayfield, L. (1999) 'The Nature and the Dilemmas of Fostering in the Nineties.' in A. Wheal (ed.) *The RHP Companion to Foster Care.* Lyme Regis: Russell House Publishing.

Ryan, T. and Walker, R. (2003) *Life Story Work: A Practical Guide to Helping Children Understand Their Past.* London: BAAF Adoption and Fostering.

Rymaszewska, J. and Philpot, T. (2006) *Reaching the Vulnerable Child. Therapy with Traumatized Children.* London: Jessica Kingsley Publishers.

Schofield, G. and Beek, M. (2006a) *Attachment Handbook for Foster Care and Adoption.* London: BAAF Adoption and Fostering.

Schofield, G. and Beek, M. (2006b) *Attachment for Foster Care and Adoption: A Training Programme.* London: BAAF Adoption and Fostering.

Schore, A. (1994) *After Regulation and the Origin of the Self.* Hillsdale, NJ: Lawrence Erlbaum Associates.

Scottish Assembly (2007) *Children Looked After 2006–2007.* www.scottishparliament.uk, accessed 11 November 2008.

Sellick, C. (1999) 'Independent fostering agencies: providing high quality services to children and carers?' *Adoption and Fostering 23, 4.*

Sellick, C. (2002) 'The aims and principles of independent fostering agencies: a view from the inside.' *Adoption and Fostering 28,* 1, pp.56–63.

Sellick, C. and Connolly, J. (2001) *National Survey of Independent Fostering Agencies.* Centre for Research on the Child and the Family, University of East Anglia.

Sellick, C., Thoburn, J. and Philpot, T. (2004) *What Works in Adoption and Foster Care?* Barkingside: Barnardo's.

Shaw, M. and Hipgrave, T. (1989) 'Specialist fostering in 1988: a research study.' *Adoption and Fostering 13, 3.*

Simon, A. and Owen, C. (2006) 'Outcomes for Children in Care. What Do We Know?' In E. Chase, A. Simon and S. Jackson (eds) *In Care and After. A Positive Perspective.* Abingdon: Routledge.

Sinclair, I. (2005) *Fostering Now. Messages from Research.* London: Jessica Kingsley Publishers.

Sinclair, I. and Gibbs, I. (1998a) *Children's Homes: A Study in Diversity.* Chichester: John Wiley & Sons.

Sinclair, I. and Gibbs, I. (1998b) *Caring for Children away from Home: Messages from Research.* London: Department of Health.

Sinclair, I., Gibbs, I. and Wilson, K. (2004) *Foster Carers: Why They Stay and Why They Leave.* London: Jessica Kingsley Publishers.

Sinclair, I., Garnett, L. and Berridge, D. (1995) *Social Work and Assessment with Adults.* London: National Children's Bureau.

Social Care Institute for Excellence (2004) *Practice Guide 3: Fostering.* London: SCIE.

Solomon, J. and George, C. (1996) 'The place of disorganization in attachment theory: linking classic observations with contemporary findings.' In J. Solomon and C. George (eds) *Attachment Disorganization.* New York, NY: Guilford Press.

Swain, V. (2007) *Can't Afford to Foster. A Survey of Fee Payments to Foster Carers in the UK.* London: Fostering Network.

Thoburn, J. (1999) 'Trends in foster care and adoption.' In O. Stevenson, O. (ed.) *Child Welfare in the UK.* Oxford: Blackwell Science.

Tomlinson, P. (2004) 'The experience of breakdown and the breakdown that can't be experienced: implications for work with traumatised children.' *Journal of Social Work Practice 22,* 1, pp.15–25.

Tomlinson, P. and Philpot, T. (2008) *A Child's Journey to Recovery. Assessment and Planning with Traumatised Children.* London: Jessica Kingsley Publishers.

Triseliotis, J., Borland, M. and Hill, M. (2000) *Delivering Foster Care.* London: British Agencies for Adoption and Fostering.

Triseliotis, J., Sellick, C. and Short, R. (1995b) *Foster Care: Theory and Practice.* London: Batsford. The authors acknowledge their debt for their historical insight to F. Davenport-Hill and F. Fowke (1989) *Children of the State.* London: Macmillan.

Triseliotis, J., Borland, K., Hill, M. and Lambert, L. (1995a) *Teenagers and the Social Work Services.* London: HMSO.

van der Kolk, B. (2002) 'In terror's grip: healing the ravages of trauma.' *Cerebrum 4,* pp.34–50.

van der Kolk, B., McFarlane, A.C. and Weisaeth, L. (1996) *Traumatic Stress: The Effects of Overwhelming Experience on Mind, Body and Society.* New York, NY: Guilford Publications.

Wagner, G. (1982) *Children of the Empire.* London: Weidenfeld & Nicolson.

Warren, D. (1997) *Foster Care in Crisis: A Call to Professionalise the Forgotten Service.* London: National Foster Care Association.

Waterhouse, S. (1997) *The Organisation of Fostering Services.* London: National Foster Care Association.

Waterhouse, S. and Brocklesby, E. (1999) *Placement Choices for Those in Temporary Foster Care.* London: National Foster Care Association.

Welsh Assembly (2001) *Social Services Statistics.* Cardiff: Welsh Assembly.

Wheal, A. and Waldeman, J. (1999) *Family and Friends as Carers: Identifying the Training Needs of Carers and Social Workers. A Research Project and Report.* London: National Foster Care Association, Unpublished.

Winnicott, D. (1966) 'The theory of the parent–child relationship.' *International Journal of Psychoanalysis 41,* pp.585–595.

Winnicott, D. (1992) *Through Paediatrics to Psychoanalysis.* London: Karnac.

Ziegler, D. (2002) *Traumatic Experience and the Brain. A Handbook for Understanding and Treating Those Traumatized as Children.* Phoenix, AR: Acacia Publishing.

The Story of SACCS

In the 1960s and 1970s professionals focused on the physical abuse (or what was called the battered baby syndrome) and neglect of children, and sexual abuse only began to gain attention in the early 1980s.

The challenge then for the social worker in child protection was to deal with this new phenomenon as part of everyday practice. They had to develop new skills to communicate with children on a subject which they, as adults, had difficulty with – that is talking about sex and their own sexuality, and, moreover, doing this in a way that could withstand, in court, the rigours of legal scrutiny.

It was at this point that Mary Walsh, now chief executive of SACCS, got together with a local authority colleague Madge Bray who was working to help disturbed children communicate by using toys. Together, they looked at how they could adapt the use of the toy box to help this very vulnerable group of children communicate their distress, especially about their abuse they had suffered. Above all, they wanted to give children a voice in decisions that would be made about them, particularly in court.

SACCS comes into being

Working within the culture of uncertainty and confusion that prevailed at the time, Mary Walsh and Madge Bray became disenchanted at the lack of time and resources available to do this work properly. They saw no alternative: in January 1987 they took it upon themselves to meet the profound needs of the deeply traumatized children whom they were seeing every day and who found themselves effectively lost and without any influence on their futures.

SACCS came into being in Madge Bray's back bedroom – the typewriter had to be unplugged to use the photocopier! Demand for the venture on which they were now embarked soon became apparent: they were inundated with requests to see children and help them to communicate about their distress. Mary Walsh and Madge Bray worked with children all over the country, helping them to tell their stories, giving comfort and allowing them to express their pain. They also acted as advocates for children in court and other decision-making bodies, and as case consultants to local authorities. Through this process, as expected, they began to notice that many of the children were changing and beginning to find some resolution to their difficulties.

They also became aware that there were some very small children who, because of what had happened to them were either too eroticized or too disturbed to be placed in foster care. Many foster carers who were not prepared or trained to deal with very challenging situations day to day would quickly become weighed down by the child's sexualized behaviour and the placement would break down. The real cause of these breakdowns was never acknowledged and, therefore, never dealt with. In time these children were labelled as unfosterable and placed in residential care along with much older children and young people.

Leaps and Bounds

The heartbreak of watching this happen to three-, four- and five-year-old children was unacceptable. The need was be able to hold the children and their behaviour lovingly, while they were helped to understand and deal with the root cause of their behaviour. The result was the setting up of Leaps and Bounds, the first SACCS residential care provision.

The birth was a long and difficult one, but after three years the first house, Hopscotch, was opened. It filled up immediately, and the children were cared for by staff trained to understand the issues and encouraged to put love into everything they did.

Many of the children placed in Leaps and Bounds had experienced many placement breakdowns; some had been placed for adoption that had subsequently failed; most had incoherent life histories; some had lost touch with members of their family; and one child, incredibly, had acquired the wrong name. The great need was to find all of this information that was lost in the system, and so the life-story service came into existence, to help to piece together the fabric of the children's lives and to give them back their own identity.

In addition, a team of professional play therapists was engaged to work with the children in Hopscotch, and subsequently at the new houses – Somersault, Cartwheel, Handstand, Leapfrog and others – while continuing to bring the special SACCS approach to children who were not in residential care.

Within SACCS, all those charged with responsibility for the well-being of the child were (and are) expected to share information with each other, so that the whole team holds the child's reality and care.

Find Us, Keep Us

The expectation at SACCS was that when children had come to terms with what had happened to them and were ready to move on, their local authorities would find foster families for them. This proved not to be the case in many instances, and children who had worked hard to recover and desperately wanted to be part of a family would have their hopes dashed. As a result their behaviour deteriorated, and it was extremely difficult to watch this happening, especially as the next part of the work needed to be done within a family.

Leaps and Bounds was never intended to become a permanent placement for the children, so looking for potential foster families and training them to care for this very challenging and vulnerable group of children became the responsibility of a new part of SACCS which was founded – Find Us, Keep Us, the fostering and family placement arm of the organization. Find Us, Keep Us became SACCS Family Placement in 2005.

Flying Colours

In 1997 Flying Colours was opened. It was a new project designed to meet the needs of young adolescents. Often these were children who had been traumatized when they were very young, but had only just started to talk about it.

As a therapist, Mary Walsh had worked with many such young people, who were not being held in a safe and contained holding environment. She knew that they often ran away when feelings overwhelmed them, and sometimes ended up living hand to mouth on inner-city streets, involved in prostitution, drug taking and worse. Flying Colours offered these young people the same loving and nurturing therapeutic care as the younger children in Leaps and Bounds, while at the same time meeting their different developmental needs.

SACCS Care

In 2003, a major rationalization was undertaken to integrate all of the SACCS services, which had evolved since the organization's early days. A new company, SACCS Care, was formed by merging Leaps and Bounds and Flying Colours. This new company provided an organizational focus on the parenting aspect of therapeutic care. This is arguably the most important job carried out with children, some of whom have similar developmental profiles to the most dangerous adults in our society. SACCS believes that unless this issue is addressed properly, traumatized children cannot have a positive experience of parenting, and when the time comes will be unable to parent their own children appropriately.

The SACCS Recovery Programme

In 2006 SACCS launched an outcomes-based approach to the treatment of traumatized children, based on the unique SACCS 24 outcomes for recovery. This programme is supported by the assessment and planning process described in this book and has achieved national recognition as an example of excellent practice (Kane 2007).

Today and tomorrow

SACCS Care is differentiated by a unique integrated model of therapeutic parenting, play therapy, life-story work and education support individually tailored to meet children's needs, coupled with a fostering service for those who are ready to move to a family.

At the time of writing, SACCS Care is a growing Midlands-based organization looking after 50 children and employing 175 professional care staff and managers. The SACCS model is underpinned by a complex structure of practice training and clinical supervision, and these standards of excellence have positioned the organization as a national leader in therapeutic care and recovery.

There are many children outside SACCS struggling with the enormous trauma caused by abuse and neglect, children whose experience has taught them that families are dangerous places in which to live. SACCS believes that every child has a right to the expert therapeutic care that can help them to recover from their emotional injuries, but for these children the specialist services they require are often not available.

The Mary Walsh Institute

By 2006 SACCS had fully evolved to offer outstanding services for children, and at this pivotal point in the company's development its practitioners found themselves increasingly called upon to lecture to, and train, fellow professionals, both nationally and internationally. Again, the time was right for SACCS to develop a new service: the Mary Walsh Institute dedicated to improving outcomes and influencing practice with traumatized children.

The institute will offer SACCS practice through a programme of higher education, vocational training, publications, research and consultancy. It now provides the foundation degree in therapeutic child care, provided by SACCS and Glyndwr University for the company's entire frontline workforce. This training ensures that all those engaged in direct work with children are full trained and professionally equipped to carry out the roles which are central to recovery. First and second degrees in therapeutic child care are in the final stages of completion with university partners. The Mary Walsh Institute was launched in 2007.

SACCS Fostering

During 2008 SACCS launched a new fostering service under the old SACCS name of Flying Colours. The aim of this service is to provide high quality placements for children who are in need of foster care. The service will establish regional centres and provide locally for children within that region. The first centre opened, in Staffordshire, at the end of 2008.

The Authors

Mike Thomas is consultant for external foster care at the Mary Walsh Institute, and has worked in social work for 25 years. He began work as a local authority social worker and transferred to specializing in foster care when he moved to Derbyshire. He later became team manager for family placement in Swindon and then lectured in family and community services at Swindon College for a year. He joined an independent fostering agency as director of family placement, where he worked for nine years. He was appointed to his present post in 2004. As well as being a social worker, Mike is also an adoptive parent and foster carer, and has been a board member of what was then the National Foster Care Association, for whom he has also worked as a trainer and contributed articles to its magazine *Foster Care*.

Terry Philpot is a writer and journalist and a contributor to a wide range of publications. He has written and edited more than a dozen books, the most recent of which are (with Anthony Douglas) *Adoption: Changing Families, Changing Times* (Routledge 2002); (with Julia Feast) *Searching Questions. Identity, Origins and Adoption* (BAAF 2003); and (with Clive Sellick and June Thoburn) *What Works in Foster Care and Adoption?* (Barnardo's 2004). He co-authored the previous four volumes of the Delivery Recovery series. In 2001, BAAF published Terry's report into private fostering, *A Very Private Practice*. He has also published reports on kinship care and two reports on residential care for older people run by the Catholic Church, the latest of which, *The Length of Days: How Can the Church Meet the Challenges of an Ageing Society?*, was published last year. He writes a column for *YoungMinds Magazine*. He is a trustee of the Social Care Institute for Excellence and of the Michael Sieff Foundation, having previously been a member of the boards of Rainer and the Centre for Policy on Ageing. He has won several awards for journalism. His latest book, *Understanding Sexual Abuse: Female Partners of Sex Offenders Tell Their Stories*, was published by Routledge last year. He is currently editing a book on residential care.

Subject Index

Author Index